Are you willing to say YES to this moment?

Vera Helleman

EFFORTLESSLY BEING yourSELF

AWAKENING IN A NEW CONSCIOUSNESS' PERSPECTIVE

1st edition, December 2014

Translation : Juul van Aken
Design : Dependance Rotterdam | Kaire Guthan
Portrait : Janine Spanjers
Print : CreateSpace

ISBN 978-1505612516

TABLE OF CONTENTS

INTRODUCTION

Have you ever noticed how unhappy people actually are? How little we laugh and really feel connected to one another? We run from pillar to post to ensure our safety and security. Keep ourselves hidden in order not to get hurt. Living a life that we really don't like. We swallow antidepressants like candy, because we feel separated from everyone, everything and from our Self, and are therefore lonely and unhappy. The real happiness we all seek, we have to this day not yet found. As long as you're still searching for more, for better or for something different, you obviously haven't found it. You have not yet found inner peace.

Many people have already discovered that being happy is not found in the outside world and thus they engage in self-examination, they have found their own way to therapy, reading self-help books or shopping around in the haven of spiritual workshops. The idea is that when we work on ourselves, we will find happiness. But all those books, courses and consultations have not brought us what we are unconsciously looking for. That's because we overlook the fact that the source of our misfortune lies in this search.

This book is written for those who have come to the end of their quest and have discovered that what they were looking for in the outside world didn't really satisfy them. This book is intended for those who move with this collective revolution. It's a step by step explanation about the functioning of the suffering human and a guide concerning the threshold of suffering to Love. It will bring about a shift in your Consciousness, and therefore in the Consciousness of us as humanity, because we are all in this together.

On all fronts there's a noticeable revolution going on in the world. The contorted ego retracts, clenches its fist against the awaking Consciousness. On the other hand seemingly more and more patterns, rules and forms no longer work and crumble, but we don't know how it can be different. There is still a lack of understanding about who we really are and how this reality works. Man is standing on the threshold of an evolutionary transition to a next level in consciousness. We awaken from the dream in which we were caught, are released from the illusions we pursued and become attuned to and aligned with the deeper layers of our Self. We are going to live from our natural state-of-being and are going to be our Self effortlessly. This means we'll make a transition from a life that is mainly undertaken at the level of the personality, led by the ego-mind in which duality prevails, to a life in accordance with our true Self which is connected to everything and everyone around it, as one consciousness.

This transition is a process. A process that will let itself be described in the following chapters. For some people, this adventure of spiritual awakening will begin with what they call a peak experience, an experience of Unity Consciousness. Others will conquer this understanding gradually. Some 'understand' it mentally although truly living the insight is not yet fully integrated. They get a glimpse of how life will be when the ego comes to rest and once again takes its place as a servant.

To prepare and guide you to the point of surrender it makes sense to understand in advance how the ego functions and how the awakened Consciousness shines through. So let's start our own Self-inquiry.

SELF-INQUIRY

...

IN THE CAR I REMEMBER THE FEELING OF A
LIFE-LONG SADNESS EVER PRESENT INSIDE ME.
I HAVE ALWAYS QUESTIONED MYSELF
WHERE THIS CAME FROM. I LOOKED FOR
ANSWERS IN PAINFUL EXPERIENCES IN MY
CHILDHOOD, LOOKED FOR REMEDIES TO
HELP THE SADNESS, SOUGHT THERAPEUTIC
HELP BUT THE DORMANT SADNESS STAYED.
BLUE ROAD SIGNS WHIZZ PAST MY VIEW.
SUDDENLY A CRYSTAL CLEAR INSIGHT ARISES.
I GRAB HOLD OF THE STEERING WHEEL
EVEN TIGHTER. FOR THE VERY FIRST TIME
I COMPLETELY UNDERSTAND WHAT THE NATURE
OF THIS SADNESS IS. IT'S THE PRIMORDIAL
SADNESS THAT I'M DISCONNECTED FROM
WHO I TRULY AM. I BURST INTO TEARS,
OVERWHELMED BY THE DESIRE
TO RETURN HOME

...

Every human being feels the pull of the Self. We've been programmed to feel the urge to seek ourSelf, which is the same as the search for Love and happiness. This is the true nature of Self. We are all searching for Love and for happiness. But because we perceive everything through the eyes of the human mind, through a human life story we search for happiness inside the story. Inside the world of time, space and form; and not by chance, it pushes us forwards. The urge to search has given us numerous experiences in this world. But true happiness can't be found in the outside world, true happiness will only be found if you look from happiness itself. From *within* yourSelf.

It's all about you finding your way back to yourSelf. To anchor in this Self, so that this new state of being can fill the rest of your life. Through yourSelf you can experience the world and give expression to yourSelf. Just *being* yourSelf! This is a revolutionary step in a human life because it means a step to the next level of consciousness. No longer in the three dimensional state where the fear and greed of the ego rules, but surpassing time, space and form to an enormous scope of experiences which unfold at your disposal, with you as the center from which everything originates in close harmony with the universe and everything in it. On this level of consciousness we will be able to access a much larger potential than we have ever dreamed of. Oneness is the obvious starting point. You're probably feeling excited already. Very good! Let this yearning for home become your guide.

In this Self inquiry we'll be addressing:

- **Who or what are we truly?**
- **What holds us back in Being ourSelf?**
  (What, are we not?)

This means that we're going to address different layers in ourself, dissected into what we call ego, the identity, the personality and what, in this book we call the Self; yourSelf, your True nature.

This process of Self-inquiry is called spiritual awakening. Awakening from the dream of who you thought you were, but you truly are not. Some people think this is a spontaneous awakening and that suddenly everything is peaceful and blissful. For some people this is the case but for the most of us it is a (sometimes) painful process of disintegration and detachment.

At the beginning you are totally asleep and unconsciously stuck in the identification with your personality and the life situations that you experience and your automatic reaction patterns. At long last you know, feel and *are* fully awakened for Who you truly are. You have insight in and work together with the laws of this reality. In this process Consciousness will shine longer and more frequently in your life and even more illusions will be punctured; increasingly more ego structures will crumble. What you are not, is coming apart at the seams.
There is a tipping of the scales about half way in this process in which you become aware that you can no longer be unfaithful to yourself. However you are still living a life based on old ego structures. Habitual behavior patterns which once gave you a sense of safety no longer work. Maybe you're there already or you haven't yet come to terms with the most difficult personality identifications. This is the most difficult phase in the process because there are no longer any escape routes to choose the safest and least painful road. This is where you will have to face your biggest fears and take steps outside your comfort zone. Luckily life starts to be a lot more fun once you've reached this turning point as the world around you begins to react to the changes within you. Everything resonates more and more with your true nature. You become visible in the world around you. Feelings of thankfulness, awe, love and joy become everyday experiences. Believe me: it's worth it!

To find out Who you truly are, you will have to know who you are not. Once the dust has been blown off your soul you will become visible. In other words: if you don't know who you are (not) you will be searching for love until the end of time. It's therefore necessary to investigate which barriers you have placed against love and to neutralize these so that Love can be freed. The path of self-inquiry is a path of detachment. Detaching yourself from the illusions of who you thought you were and what you thought you needed. That's the reason why we're starting with an intensive investigation into the nature of the ego. Once this mechanism is totally seen through you will no longer be stuck in the suffering mode and the separation which is part of it. You move to the position of the Self which is connected to the body and spirit; to everything.

Self-inquiry covers these four areas so that consciousness can filter through all facets of life and you can reach spiritual maturity.

- **Your relationship with yourSelf**
- **Your relationship with 'the other'**
- **Your relationship with your physical body and the manifest**
- **Your relationship and service to the field of Unity**

In the following chapters we will begin with the relationship with yourSelf, from which everything originates.

Because this book came to you, I assume that you are ready to make the step from an ego-led life to effortlessly *being*, in tune with, and connected to your true Self.
Everything which manifests in your life is in service to this process because it is the natural way back to yourself. Coincidence doesn't exist (in no-thing). Are you ready to take a leap into the infinite mystery, and do you need some help with this, then life will give you teachers. Maybe this book will be your teacher for the coming period of time.

PART I

YOUR RELATIONSHIP

WITH YOURSELF

IDENTIFICATION

EVERYTHING
WE MAKE 'ME'
KEEPS US AWAY
FROM THE DIRECT EXPERIENCE
OF
THIS
MOMENT

Straight to the chase, our reality is based on the experience of separation due to the fact that we are not conscious of the true nature of the ego. The nature of the human mind is egoic. From a very early age, we are already defining who we are. We define our sex, our name, our qualities, our possessions and ideas. Once we find something we're content with, we want to claim it. The object we want becomes 'mine'; my partner, my car, my theory, my athletic body. And even things we are not happy with will get a 'my' label; my problem, my illness, my overweight body, my sister's illness, my sensitivity.

Having a 'my' (mine) label gives us our identity and sense of self. I'm someone with a good figure, brilliant ideas, a rich inner world but I have a terrible life. The 'my' mechanism, which is the ego, always wants to better everything. It's never ok with what IS. It *wants.* It wants better, it wants more, and it wants something else or wants *nothing* at all. Whatever it does or doesn't want, the ego's motivation to remain wanting is to strengthen its identity, its life force. It doesn't even matter whether it's a positive or negative identity; the goal of the my-mechanism is to reinforce the ego.

An über-me (a superior me) or an unter-me (an inferior me), through a success story or a drama, a Me is a Me. Problems in themselves can be particularly good at giving a big dose of me-ness because problems, in the exchange with others are pre-eminently a source of attention and therefore food for the me. Problems reaffirm the 'me' and 'mine'. In whichever form problems come, they appropriate attention and feed the little 'me'.

Another component of 'me' is 'yours'. Comparing yourself to others is a ploy to strengthen your identity. My ideas are more idealistic, better and more intelligent than yours. My problems are much worse and far more exceptional than yours. The 'me' we distinguish ourselves from others with, is the my-mechanism that will do anything to keep its identity intact. Or in other words the 'me' which separates us from others, especially from our true Self. Separation and duality are our common reality. Everything you 'own' keeps you a prisoner in duality.

The minute you make something 'mine' you lay claim to it and as a result you feel the fear of losing it. The fear of losing something holds the bow tightly strained in order to keep it intact and to keep control. It makes you feel uneasy and cramped, anything but relaxed. If you turn it around: everything you make 'mine' but don't want (like a bad feeling or an illness) will keep you constantly occupied to rid yourself of it. However, since you have made it 'mine', you will never be free of it.

And take, for example that you've made someone 'mine' who you think will make you happy, then you consequently want to determine what happens to this 'mine'. But you can never control another person. If you do try this, the love will leak away and will lose its spontaneity.

The irony of all this is, once you see through the my-mechanism, is that the other and therefore duality no longer exists. It's an illusion. There is only complete unity. Because everything in this reality is transitory. Eventually all of the 'mine' will disappear. This 'you' that you have built up, with the aid of this mechanism is nothing more than a bundle of materialized ideas.

The my-mechanism also creates 'my' feelings. If a feeling comes up, that looks like sadness then it also makes it 'mine'. And the 'mine' gets a story, a cause and an effect 'that's because this and that happened to me.' 'The nasty feeling has to disappear because it's not a nice feeling.' You're fighting against something which would never have been a problem if you hadn't made it 'mine'.

A lot of people are unsure of themselves, unsure of the 'me' they've created inside their head. With one person the insecurity lies in not being able to comply with expectations and with another it's the way they look or something else. Take a normal day: You're having a bad hair day and the clothes you chose make you look chubbier than you would like, but that's how it is.

You haven't accepted your chubbiness, but you comply with the body you have. You walk through a shopping mall, and on the other side a man looks at you with raised eyebrows. At least, it seems that way. Immediately your my-mechanism gets activated. That look is about me. He thinks I look silly. You feel a cramp of disapproval in your stomach. You look away and see a beautiful, slender lady walking by.

You immediately start to compare. The 'my-your' mechanism is fully active.
You can probably recognise a similar situation with yourself. Denying yourself makes you unhappy. That's logical because intuitively we know that we were meant to shine. The core of this miserable spiral into suffering is the moment that you stuck 'mine' on what you saw. Your body, how the other person looked at you, the stare and the passer-by were compared with the 'me'. So answer this question: Are you your body? Or are you the one who lives in your body, who uses it and experiences through it?

It's all about seeing through this constantly active identification mechanism. So, this means that on your path to awakening you develop vigilance, that you stay alert to the invasion of the ego. That you keep a sharp eye out for all the subtle thoughts, feelings and experiences through which the 'my-mechanism' is activated. This is where your chance at freedom lies. The mind remains. It's an illusion that it will disappear. As long as you wander around in this reality the ego is present. But if you stay vigilant then the ego will, as soon as it pops up, be seen through and will therefore stay in its position in service of you instead of taking you over. The 'my-mechanism" recedes and therefore you enter inner peace. Or, as it is often said in Eastern manuscripts; the 'you' dies. The images and ideas you had about yourself cease to exist. An enormous liberation!

SOURCE OF LIFE

WHO WOULD YOU BE
IF WHAT YOU IDENTIFY
YOURSELF WITH
FALLS AWAY?

WHO WOULD BE LEFT
IF ALL YOUR IDEAS
ABOUT YOURSELF
DISAPPEAR?

WHAT REMAINS
UNCHANGED AND ALL PRESENT
WHEN YOUR SEARCHING
STOPS?

Shut your eyes after reading this and permit yourself, if only for a moment to let go of all the searching, all the wanting, all the 'mine' and 'me' and to become aware of what becomes visible beyond the focus. Without attaching labels. Feel the life that flows through you. At times as a soft murmur and suddenly wildly careering through your body and beyond. The life in you is always moving, neither placid nor inhibited. See if you can observe what's moving in and through you without attaching value to anything. Become aware how life is pulsating through you, like the waves of an ocean. Your feelings come up and then they return back to the source of their origin.

You are the only one able to perceive this, as you are the Source out of which everything originates. The Source of Life. Your body's senses allow you to be aware of this manifestation of Source, in the form of you. In relation to everything that manifests you are the unequivocal observer; an unwritten, open space. Your true nature is Love. Is Life. Is Acceptance.
You are endless Consciousness, God; the creator *and* the creature who experiences this. You are the space in which yin and yang dance together. You are the deep stillness, the ever existing peace behind every story which unfolds in the world of form. Who you really are cannot be touched by pain or sadness as it is this source that has enabled pain and sadness to come into existence and to be experienced.
Everything takes place *inside* you in the infinite Now, which is Love. Everything is Love, everything is You, and everything is Now. You are simultaneously everything and nothing. You are all that existed before this story and that will live on after physical death. What you are is impossible to put into words as it is wordless, formless, me-less. The beating Heart of the universe where everything fits into place. You!

For some people this can be pretty vague ;) Or too good to be true - Which is totally logical! Because putting into words Who you are is just impossible. It can't be known. But what am I seeking if I can never find mySelf? This is a paradox in itself and I'll let you see why:

IT'S NOT ABOUT
YOU FINDING YOURSELF
BUT ABOUT
BEING
YOUR(TRUE)SELF

IT'S NOT ABOUT
LOOKING AT YOURSELF
BUT
STARTING TO LOOK
FROM YOURSELF

Can you feel the difference here?

It's a change of perspective. The mechanism which continuously identifies and compares itself with the outside world which plays tiresome games will stop if your perspective changes. So don't look at yourself but look from yourSelf. Be in a state of total acceptance, no longer punishing or judging yourself and finding that judgements and fixations no longer even arise. You look beyond your personality, from yourself at the reflections of yourself.

It's really just a small shift in perspective, but a huge transition for mankind.

THOUGHTS

THINKING
IS NOT THE PROBLEM

TAKING THE THOUGHT
SERIOUSLY
IS

We see and experience this life through the personality and we identify with this personality. This means that we are trapped in a limited body, with limited ideas about who we are. Let's zoom in on the thought-factory that produces all these ideas.

Everything in this reality begins with a thought. 'And then, there was word'. Every thought you believe in becomes a small package of beliefs which determine how you view yourself and how you relate to the world around you. The term 'belief system' gives an accurate account of this mechanism within us: A collection of thoughts which you believe in and continue believing in. Because of this you keep on projecting these beliefs on the outside world, as the outside world is a product of your conscious and unconscious belief system. That's what's meant by the term 'the cycle of rebirth'. All those beliefs are projected anew, as a hologram in every Now. Stopping with believing in these thoughts and choosing to be here and Now is a step out of the cycle of rebirth. It is the transition to another dimension, another state-of-Being.

Suffering is a consequence of believing in thoughts, we make the thought 'mine'. Suffering is unnecessary; if you examine a thought meticulously you will see that a thought never encompasses the real reality. A thought is always about then or when and never about Now. Worrying is a collection of thoughts about 'what-can-maybe-happen-to-me-or-mine-if... ' Often the fear of suffering is worse than suffering itself. Take for instance the birthday calendar on which the date of your mother's birthday is written. If you look at this objectively you will only see blue ink on paper. However, nothing in this world is objective, your human mind continually slides between your perceptions and very quickly the blue ink on paper becomes "Hm, a present. But what can I give someone who has everything. We're living in a disposable consumer society; all that waste is terrible, yuck. Oh, and then her friend will probably also be at the party. She always knows how to press my buttons, she's so self-centered'. And so on and so on. Within a few seconds, 30 thoughts have passed by, a few of which have already trapped you. We lose ourSelf in the content of a succession of thoughts. In the example you can identify a number of beliefs:
someone is having a birthday, you have to visit and you're expected to take a present; you hate consumerism and self-centeredness. Thinking of yourself first is wrong and it didn't even occur to you to ask yourself if you wanted to attend the party or not. On the mind level we are so

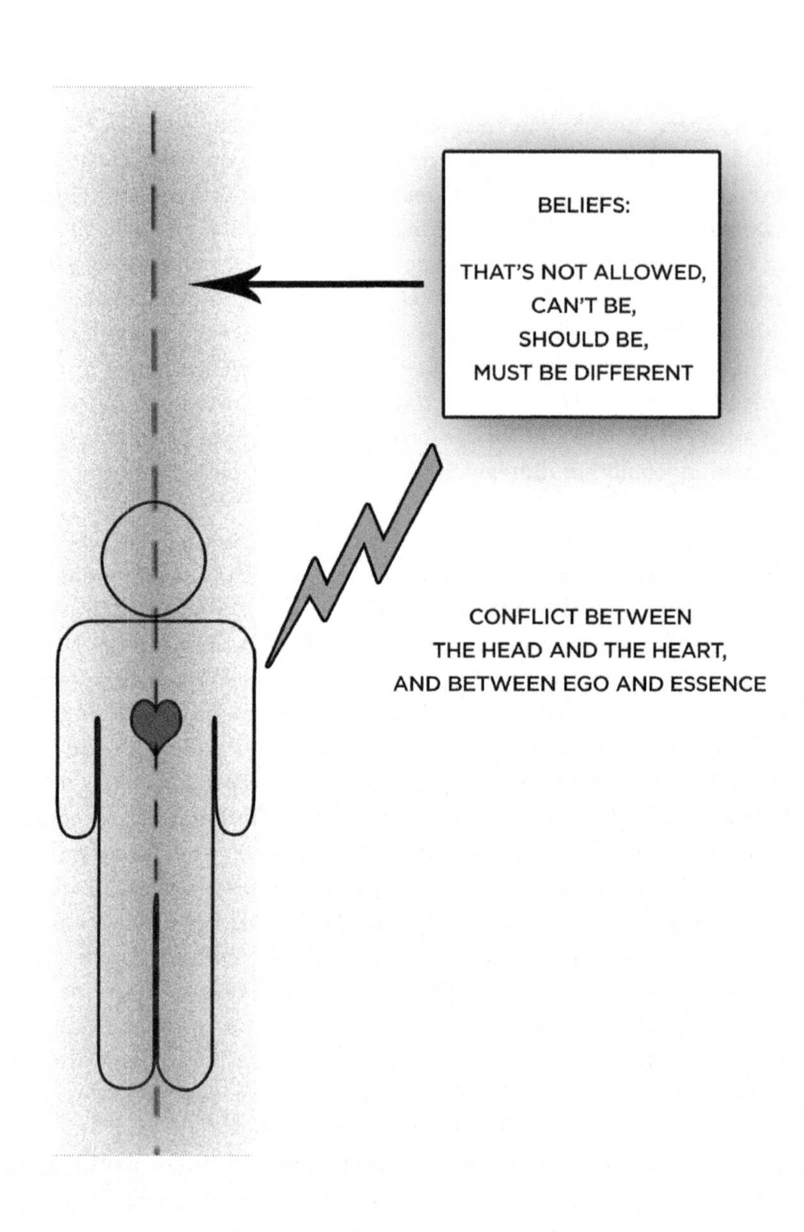
BELIEFS:
THAT'S NOT ALLOWED,
CAN'T BE,
SHOULD BE,
MUST BE DIFFERENT
CONFLICT BETWEEN
THE HEAD AND THE HEART,
AND BETWEEN EGO AND ESSENCE

programmed by our upbringing, by the media, by the pressure of society and our successes and failures that we are no longer autonomous. We are completely enslaved by our belief system. The question is, is this belief system serving ourSelf or serving the continuation of the 'my' and 'me'-mode that feels safe within an ego directed society?

You as Essence had the intention to experience certain things. Most ideally these experiences would be able to develop, if you were truly yourSelf, but instead you're sabotaged by your belief system. Belief systems don't usually align with your Essence, with Who you truly are. And thus, once a situation arises and activates your belief system a conflict between your head and your heart, between ego and Essence, also arises. And believe me, with our limited thought patterns we can't oversee what the incentive of our Essence is. The heart has reasons the head doesn't understand. One thing's for sure: if you contradict your heart... you always lose!

This belief system can also be called your comfort zone. Once there was a good reason to make certain beliefs your own. They made you feel safe and secure. Living by these rules, protected your being 'someone'. Beliefs are a product of the my-mechanism. Beliefs are formed in this world from an early age and are based on survival. If I am nice and kind then I will be given food, attention and love. It was necessary to be able to function here, so there's no reason why you should punish yourself for it. What I would like to do is to invite you to take a good look and see if you still need these beliefs Now. Neutralizing your beliefs will bring you freedom and help you grow to spiritual maturity.

Most beliefs are based on the childlike desires to be found kind and loveable by mummy or daddy and later by your partner, or being seen and heard and receiving recognition from the outside world. Other beliefs develop later and are based on the fear of losing what we thought would give us happiness or a livelihood, our house, our job, our partner, our image. In short: our belief system is the framework that secures all of the 'mine'. The rules which tell us how to act without losing the 'me' and the world with which we identify ourselves.

It's a big step in your spiritual development when you throw away your own rules and your belief system; when you take steps outside your comfort zone. This is the way you can regain access to the unlimited love of the great Heart.

Let's take a look at our thoughts in even more detail now. How true are the thoughts you believe in really? Could they be something different? Can I be absolutely sure that they are true? And what would remain if I no longer believed in them?
If we take the last example we can ask ourselves the question if thinking about yourself first, is really wrong or not. You probably had this confirmed by the outside world time and time again when you were young.
Thoroughly investigate its true reality. What if you think about yourself first? What then? Wouldn't you truly be a lot happier and thus a shining, enjoyable company for others? Is it really necessary to put yourself on the back burner to please someone else? Are you absolutely sure that this is what the other needs? Can you truly know what someone else needs at all? Are you responsible or are you taking over someone's autonomy? Then, is it not really egoistic to think that you know what someone else needs and to feel good about yourself because of what you did for the other person? Maybe if you think about yourself first, then act and for example not go to the party, you could give someone a really good chance to reflect on themselves. It could just be that what the group dynamics needs (without your irritation), is what everyone needs and knew all along on the level of Essence. Or maybe...
...I could carry on for a while longer. Because really, your resistance to egoism, is your repressed desire to think a lot more about yourself first! In order to *be* yourself, you have to let the belief become completely free. For every belief finds its echo in the outside world.

It is tempting, when investigating a belief, to turn it into a new truth, for example 'by thinking of myself I help someone else'. But then you'll be stuck in a new belief; will you let yourself help someone if it is needed or are you so determined that saying 'no' is the best option (because thinking about yourself first is in fact helping the other?) Don't go jumping to any new conclusions!
With every new conclusion you trap yourself in the ego. Interpreting and interfering in the flow of life! Let every Now stand in its own right. Every moment is different. The situation is different, you are different, as is the other person. When you investigate and look at a belief, look beyond. Is there anything you can absolutely know for sure? No. In

principal, every thought is blank, it only obtains truth if you give it value.

What would happen if you let every belief about good or bad, what may or may not be, or what should and shall be, go. What would remain?

...INNER PEACE...

SPACE...

FREEDOM...

FREEDOM IS A CHOICE!

DO YOU CHOOSE
TO GO INTO A THOUGHT
OR
DO YOU REMAIN RECEPTIVE
IN EVERY NEW NOW?

You are not your thoughts. You are the observer of your thoughts. Thoughts think themselves and you choose whether or not to follow and believe in a thought when it comes up! Yes, it's that simple. You choose which thought you make the truth and you will see that not one thought is worthy of losing the connection with yourself (which is what happens once you start believing in a thought). It pulls you out of the Now. It disconnects you from yourSelf. Thoughts arise out of nothing and disappear back into nothing... just as long as you don't attach to them. Thoughts really aren't the problem, they can even be very entertaining. That's why you don't have to fight them. This only reverses the problem, because everything you abhor, grows. The invitation is clearly to no longer make them 'mine' any more.

Constant vigilance is necessary to keep out of the clutches of the ego. If the pull of the story you identify yourself with is too strong, it will require enormous courage. The courage to turn your back on your beliefs. The courage to look all your fears in the eye and to stop trying to be right, to lose face.

We've discovered that every drama begins by believing in a thought. The moment a thought arises and you feel resistance (because you believe in the thought) you have a choice! Provided you're awake in that moment. As long as you're asleep you're unable to choose.

When you see through the my-mechanism and know that all contortions in the form of emotions are a result of believing in thoughts and making the story 'mine', then you can go in two directions.

- **You can follow the thought,** and by associating with it follow every thought that follows, which in turn brings emotions and even more thoughts......and even more emotions, and then end up in an emotional vortex, locked in this world of duality.
- **Or you can say 'NO',** I'm not making these thoughts 'mine'. I will permit everything which arises in the here and Now to be and stay firmly rooted in the here and Now; in connection with myself as Essence. ONE with all that IS.

What you choose essentially is to no longer step into the ego-cramp. So you adopt an attitude of 'non-doing'. Of non interfering in what you

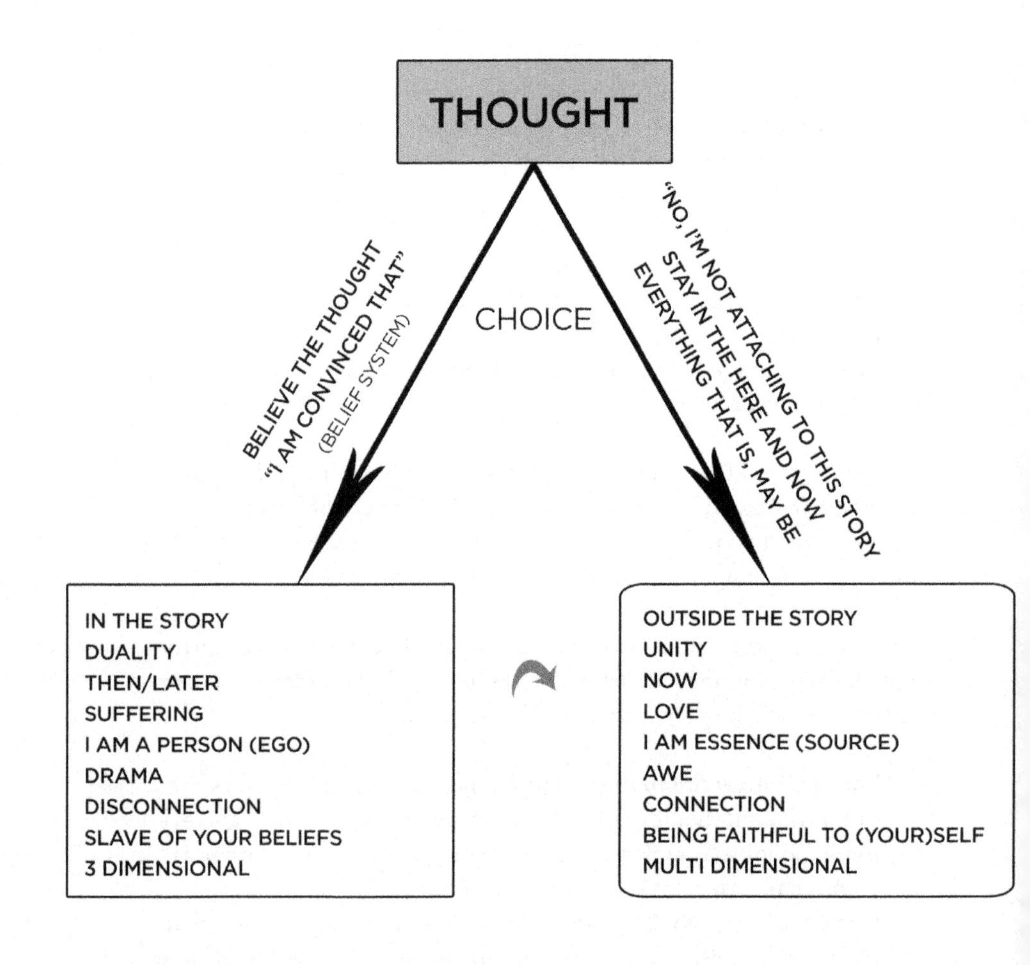
THOUGHT
CHOICE
BELIEVE THE THOUGHT
"I AM CONVINCED THAT"
(BELIEF SYSTEM)
"NO, I'M NOT ATTACHING TO THIS STORY
STAY IN THE HERE AND NOW
EVERYTHING THAT IS, MAY BE
IN THE STORY
DUALITY
THEN/LATER
SUFFERING
I AM A PERSON (EGO)
DRAMA
DISCONNECTION
SLAVE OF YOUR BELIEFS
3 DIMENSIONAL
OUTSIDE THE STORY
UNITY
NOW
LOVE
I AM ESSENCE (SOURCE)
AWE
CONNECTION
BEING FAITHFUL TO (YOUR)SELF
MULTI DIMENSIONAL

as Essence wanted to live and you surrender yourself to yourSelf as Consciousness.

Non-doing is not the same as not-doing (doing nothing). This sometimes gets misconstrued. Doing nothing is impossible because there is always movement between action and rest. What I mean by not-doing is to see how the my-mechanism is always busy trying to make something else of what IS, instead of experiencing what Is. Non-doing is giving up your resistance to what IS, no longer interpreting, grabbing, identifying, labeling, associating and drawing conclusions. We stop trying to make static that what is always in motion. We stop investing in and chasing after illusions!

Choosing no longer to believe in your thoughts is seeing your futility as a personality and realizing that you as Consciousness are the only one present.

EMOTIONS

HOW
DOES
THE EGO
HANDLE
FEELINGS?

You experience yourSelf through a body with thoughts and feelings. Your identification with this lets you function on the level of a person who is seeking either more good feelings or less unpleasant feelings.

To avoid pain or to gain pleasure

The feelings we label as positive are not seen as a problem, it's the negative feelings we would rather leave aside.
If a thought arises in your consciousness and you give it worth your emotional body will react immediately (such as a thought about something nice which in turn makes good feelings arise). But mostly, the thoughts we give worth are of a different kind, for example the thought that you're not looking forward to something, anticipating something, (and again it's a thought) because a similar situation in the past didn't turn out well. That's when your emotional system cramps up and you say ' I'm tense', 'I am scared' or 'I am sad'.

The ego, i.e. the mind, uses two ways to handle negative emotions:

1. **It *suppresses* the sensation and hides it away in Pandora's box**

2. **Or it *expresses* the emotion, releasing it into the outside world**

Both movements are a movement away from what is truly taking place at this moment on a deeper level of yourself. The ego, by repressing the feeling, will ignore what is screaming to be seen and will therefore keep intact the story behind it, because emotions and stories are linked and thus again are not seen through.

This results in an emotional blockage in your energy system and you will then experience the separation with yourSelf. On the other hand, the ego can also act out its discontent on others; on people or animals around it and live in resistance and isolation from the outside world. Because outside is inside and the other way around, you will also feel the separation with yourself when acting out emotions. Both strategies eventually lead to duality and therefore, to suffering.

Emotions really don't have to be a struggle, they were never designed for this. The identification with emotions is very trying for many of us, because they seem so real. You feel something and your body even reacts. But, you are not your emotions, you are not your thoughts and not your body. You are the observer of your emotions!
Your emotions are a response to a thought and therefore a memory of a thought you believed in. The quicker you locate an emotion, the closer you're to the thought that began the drama: 'I have to do something that I don't like'. Your emotions help you to look at the truth behind them and to stay vigilant to the pull of the ego.

Do you want to take the step to live your natural state of being and to connect with yourSelf, then it's very important that you give up the resistance to 'negative' emotions. And also the resistance to enjoyment which you're not allowed to feel. As long as you stay in resistance to pain and discomfort the emotion that is now present in your system (and your resistance!) will stay and grow and bring you out of connection with yourSelf.

But ... there is another way to deal with troublesome emotions:

3. Let the sensation fully be...

Receive it for 100%. By letting go of your resistance something wonderful will happen. Your heart opens (your heart chakra), your connection to the unified field of endless possibilities opens (your crown) and your connection to the earth opens (base chakra) as will all the chakras in between. I've seen this happen time and time again with people who were prepared to be receptive to what arises within their energy system. When these centers are opened you become an open channel in which the emotion can be experienced and subsequently transformed. This transformation is a natural occurrence. Love transforms all darkness into light. You feel that the emotion whirls around for a few seconds and then dissolves into awareness. It's very important when speaking about freedom that you remain in the position of the observer. This is the only place to stay out of emotional drama and stay firmly rooted in the here and now.
To meet feelings in this way can be very scary for some people. Scary, because it can seem that you're being swallowed up by despair, or that a big box of unprocessed shit has been opened over which you have

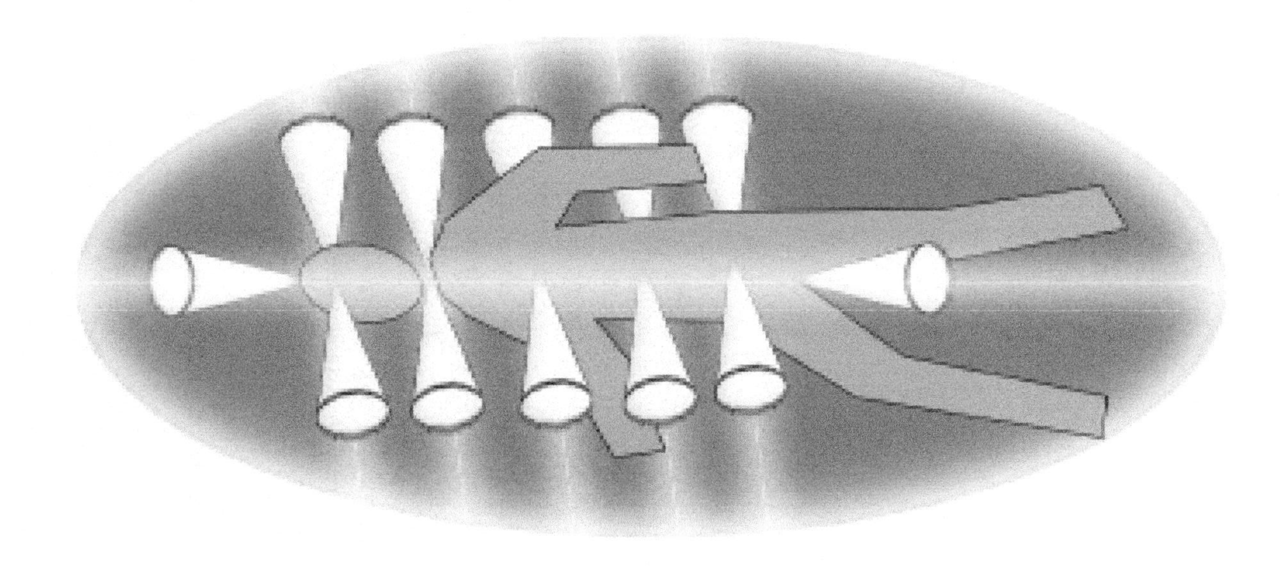

no control. Many people find their nervous system is not yet aligned to cope with so much intensity. That's why it takes a while to get used to this intensity and let it be. In the end every sensation that is totally allowed to be, is a gateway to the never ending Now. It's your ability to be receptive; that will decide if you can go through this gateless gateway.

Psychology speaks of four basic emotions: fear, anger, sadness and happiness. Some people add aversion, envy and amazement to this list. And yet others say that there are only two basic emotions: fear and love. According to me the energy flow in the emotional body cannot be defined because there are millions in every Now and they are all different. Nothing feels exactly like it did before. Everything is energy and constantly in movement. It's the same as sound. When you hear the sound of a triangle for instance then the sound vibrates into your energy system and dissolves...just as long as you don't make the sound 'mine'. It's the same with feelings. A sensation vibrates into your energy field and vibrates out of it when you, as observer, receptively observe. If you try and label the energy then you take a step back into the world of concepts, into your mind. That's what we're now leaving behind. If the sensation is totally allowed to be it will be transformed. The key is being 100% lovingly open to every energy sensation that reveals itself to you.

THE GATEWAY TO THE NOW

EACH SENSATION
IS A POSSIBILITY
TO CHOOSE
THE INFINITE MYSTERY
OF THIS MOMENT

Every sensation is a gateway to the Now.
The human manifestation contains a number of energy levels in different vibrational bandwidths, some of which I will discuss and elaborate. All of these levels are connected to our earthly reality and therefore to the personal(ity):

1. **the spiritual body**
2. **the mental body**
3. **the emotional body**
4. **the physical body**

The manifest, the outside world, is a projection of the personal as well as the collective consciousness. I will cover this further on in this book. The spotted line in the figure on the next page gives you an indication of the channel that connects the spiritual body with the omnipresent Consciousness.

95% of the emotions of a human being, who wholly identifies with his/her personality are a result of the belief in a thought. 5% of the human feelings are the mouth piece of your Essence and give information about what IS. Or in other words, for 95% you are the plaything of your emotions; a result of believing in a story.and 5% of which is transparent enough for your Self to pierce through your sabotage barrier and lead you to where you as Essence need to go. Once the process of awakening has begun, when you start living from your Self then this ratio will turn around and eventually become 100% promptings from Source and will no longer be emotion led. That is the shift.

We can therefore see a difference between emotions and feelings!

- **Emotions** are reactions within your emotional body as a result of making a thought (from the mental body) 'mine'.
- **Feelings** are sensations which arise from the spiritual body (or light body) and are felt in the energy field in and around you. In experiencing these sensations there is no judgment and no 'me' attachment, only an experience and propulsion in the Now.

Most of the time we are not even aware of the thought that preceded the emotion. That's why we're going to implement sensations as a wakeup call. We're going to stop digging around in the world of thought and

start focusing on sensations. This will give us a big advantage in terms of awakening.
All sensations, whether experienced via your eyes, nose, ears, your body or your feeling-nature, are a gateway to the Now. If a sensation is fully observed and allowed to be, it opens the heart and therefore the connection to your Self, to Unity.

A natural result of this process is that your feeling nature will develop and sharpen as your fine tuning to subtler energy fields expands.
This is how you can reach beyond the 3D world and begin to feel the true energy flow present in the here and now. It opens a door to a whole new reality; one in which a new adventure unfolds every moment and where changes in the energy flow become visible in the manifest.

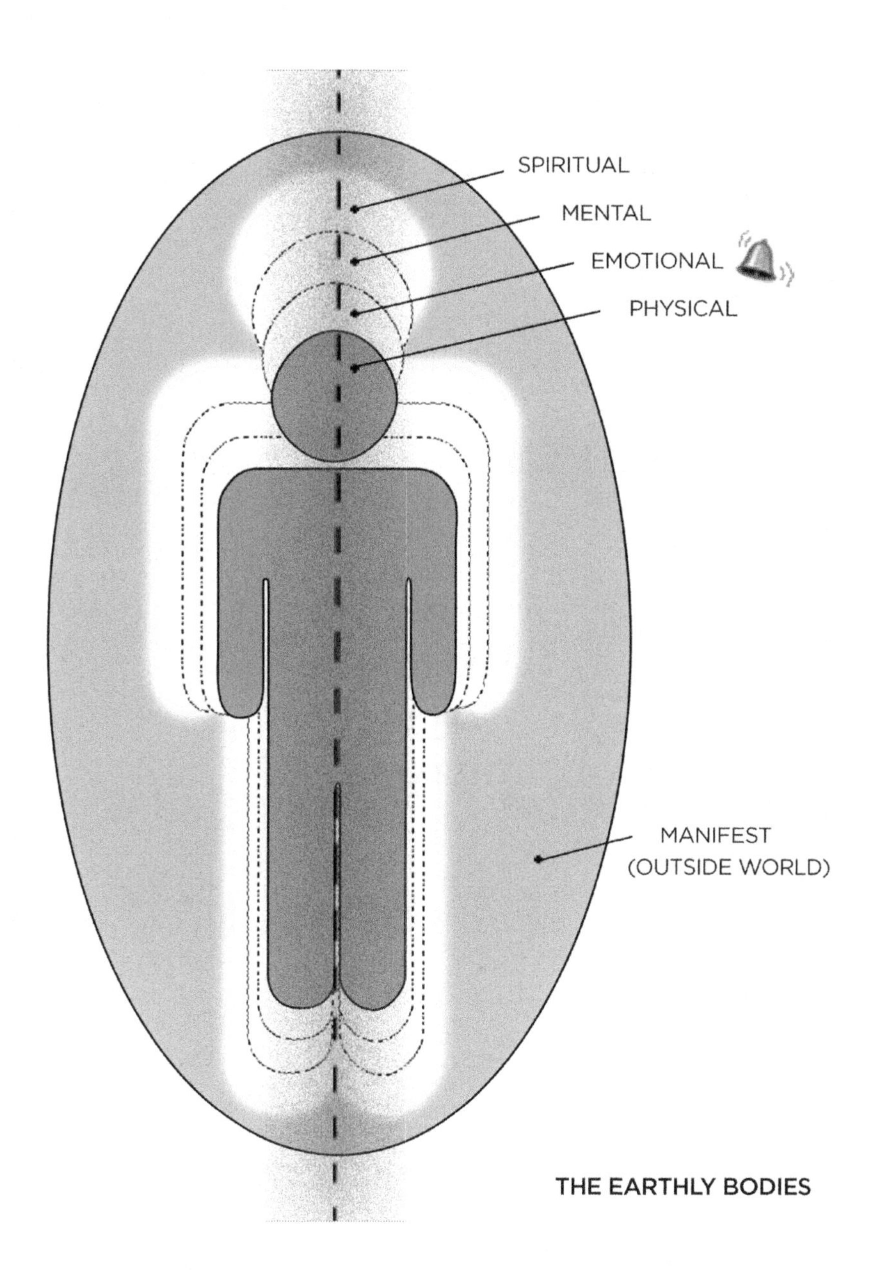

THE EARTHLY BODIES

DEFENCE MECHANISMS

HOW
DO YOU
AVOID
THE NOW?

You'll find that it's not always easy to let everything just be and to let everything flow through you. Often we can't even connect with what we feel, which is completely logical as since childhood we've been taught all sorts of tricks to avoid unpleasant feelings. These tricks are called our defence mechanisms. We have become so good at this that we completely own them and in many people they are 'on' all the time. Therefore we are no longer aware that we are continually shutting ourself off. By shutting off we have lost the connection with our Self. Defence mechanisms were created because at the time it seemed this was the best method to protect our Self. They are frequently activated when we find ourselves in emotionally tense situations, when we think we have to hide our sincerely stricken Self because we are not OK about what has become visible about us. For example when you're the center of attention and still unsure about who you are, or if you get asked to do something and you want to do it well but you feel disapproval. Or even when you feel hurt because what you expected doesn't happen or when you're triggered in old pain issues. But is this really still necessary? Do you need this defence mechanism once you fully comprehend that Who you really are cannot be hurt? That only the image of who you thought you were starts to crumble. We believe in our thoughts and *we defend a bundle of ideas about who we think we are and what will happen if....* And that's why a defence mechanism, once you awaken from the dream, is solely a way to hide our Self.

Therefore it's very useful to be aware of your favorite defence mechanism. Why? Because you can be vigilant for it and have access to the choice in the figure. Usually there's a step between; if you find yourself caught up in a defence mechanism, when you 'freeze', there's such a big shield around you that it makes the gateway to the Now seem very far away, then:

Be prepared to observe
your thoughts as well as your feelings!

As a defence mechanism is also energy and always moving, you can welcome it as a sensation. So if you are prepared to observe it, you will let go of your fearful ego and the 'avoiding the Now' can make its way back to Source. You will gradually move to the position of observer and choose whether or not to attach to the thought that preceded your free-zing up and go with it, or to stay present in the here and now.

Let's look closely at a few defence mechanisms:

- **Rationalizing**
  A well-used method by people in our western society. Which is logical as this ego controlled society always wants a *reason*, an explanation for your thoughts, actions and feelings. We continually debate why we should or shouldn't do something or about what we've already done. We condone what we feel, ignoring it with statements and thoughts which deny our humanity. We're not conscious of the fact that rationalizing is always about then and later. Everything takes place around your interference. By rationalizing we lie to ourselves, as per definition, moving into the rational mind and believing in illusions is the path away from Self.

- **Withdrawal**
  What I see happening in the energy field of a person who withdraws is that the presence in the body (and thus in the here and Now) disappears. The energy field of the person becomes so transparent that it is no longer visible. You then literally experience that other people no longer acknowledge you because your light is no longer visible. We also call this dissociation, or retracting from the body; becoming invisible. This is often the case in the world of 'spirituality' as it's a favorite mechanism used by people with a sensitive nature.

- **Forming Reactions**
  In order not to feel the now, or in other words to conceal from ourselves and from the outside world that we've been triggered (by something or someone) we immediately and automatically react by giggling, making jokes, trying to be cool or by taking on a particular stance. In other words, shifting your attention behind a safe mask which you think will protect you.

- **Projection**
  When a nasty emotion results in a drama, this defence mechanism attributes the emotion to someone or something outside our self. For many people this is such a repetitive pattern that an emotion will always immediately be labeled and the cause of it sought outside oneself. This way, you don't have to feel yourself. You don't

accept what arises in the here and now within you. That's how you create duality; not me, but the other. And duality is suffering.

- **Repression**
  Some people have many painful feelings and memories about the past which they've fully repressed. This often occurs with traumatic experiences. We can't remember anything anymore as the memory and the experience have been tightly hidden away in our brain. You might think that what doesn't repeat isn't yours, but this isn't the case. What you've repressed does indeed have an effect and an influence. Repression or dissociating is a not being able or willing to look at dramatic 'repressed' emotions. But trust that this will, at the right time arise once again in another situation, often touching on the same pain but in a milder way. These situations will keep on repeating themselves until you are willing to observe what it is that has hidden itself in seclusion.

Waking up from the dream and slowly aligning yourself to Who you truly are can't be forced. Insights will come when you're ready for them. Noticing your own defence mechanisms will only happen when you're ready to see through them. Trust in yourSelf, as everything in life comes at the right time. Freely being yourSelf is only possible when you're prepared to be completely naked. When you don't have to protect anything anymore!

The moment you surrender to the Self all false security and false beliefs will disappear. You then realize that you were chasing after illusions. Nothing can be controlled and You don't need to be protected. Being completely naked is very scary for many people because it seems like the carpet gets tugged right out from under your feet. You step into the uncertainty of not knowing if what you know is still there; no longer knowing if your partner will stay with you, or if you will keep your job; or... This doesn't mean that you're going to lose all of this. Everything fits into place. It's all about your being prepared to let everything go, to let it free, to experience and feelingly observe. Only then can you take the step out of the ego mode into a life with an open heart. As long as you hold onto security and stability this step is not possible.

THE OBSERVER

BUT
IF I'M NOT
WHO I ALWAYS
THOUGHT I WAS...

WHO AM I?

A quick resume. We're all inhabiting a human jacket of thoughts and feelings. What makes humanity difficult to live with, is that we identify with our humanity. If we become vigilant of this mechanism, we can choose not to believe in these identifying thoughts, to not make them 'mine', but to stay present in the here and now, allowing everything that arises to be. But even so, the mystery will still exist. Then who am I? Wasn't this about returning back to yourSelf?

It's impossible to describe who we really are. We are the unmentionable, but I can describe how awakened consciousness manifests through you... When the my-mechanism is seen for what it is and 'you' surrender to the Self, or in other words: you become one with yourSelf, then your heart opens. Then there is a continuous outward flow of Love. Into everything and everyone around you, because at this level there is no difference between loving someone less or more. This is unconditional Love. A love that IS; without needing something to happen, without you needing to know the person.
In the connection with yourSelf there is trust (read; certainty) that everything in life matches, because you understand how this reality works. If you are in connection *with* yourSelf you are automatically in connection *with* the other and the world around you. There is thankfulness for life because you have realized that you wanted to be here. There is awe because everything is always new and the mystery always does its work. You feel inspired because you are plugged into the unified field of endless possibilities. There is compassion and total acceptance of yourSelf and everything around you because this is the core who you really are. There are no judgments because your true self is not polarized. There is openness and sincerity because there is nothing to protect any more. The playfulness of a child. Inner peace and silence. And the enormous freedom you always knew existed, because you *are* freedom. It is simply experiencing the world in all its polarity without labeling something good or bad. Therefore it is no longer a suffering but being in awe about the flow of life.

All of this is not who you are! But what you experience when you move out of the ego mode. Here it comes: You're able to experience this... because you are the *observer*. You're the observer who looks through the eyes of the vessel which you house, in this reality.

Everything you see, hear, feel, smell and taste is a projection.
A projected image which you can see but not what you are. This is only possible because there is distance between you and every projection under the sun, and you are the all observing. An eye can see everything but itself. A tongue can taste everything but itself. You can experience everything because you are not that which you experience, only what you experience as the observer. Everything you feel distance to cannot be you.

When you consciously take on the position of observer you are no longer imprisoned by the ego!
You've then made the shift to another perspective of consciousness. Once this insight fully realizes itself in you, then duality is past. You are the observer, the absolute middle point; non-polar. And you look through the body which you temporarily inhabit, you hear through its ears, taste with its tongue, feel with its energy field... and therefore a very special world has become available to you. The world of duality, the most incredible projection that exists!
In this process of transition you may notice that you haven't yet fully switched to this viewpoint and are therefore still in identification and suffering. But, remind yourself, when you consciously become the observer you will no longer be imprisoned by the ego. If you don't react then you're still sleeping, if you're conscious of your defence mechanisms, then you have a choice! Are you going to believe in; this is 'my' problem, 'my' challenge, 'my' sadness, or do you remain lovingly observing, feeling the space where everything is okay, so that the concepts release you.

ARE YOU SURE?

THERE IS NOTHING
I KNOW FOR SURE

ONLY
THAT
I
EXIST

Your true Self wants to become visible through you, through this human manifestation. But as long as the ego interferes and as long as you depend on a limiting belief system which isn't aligned with Who you are, your Self cannot break through. The mind, the ego, the glasses you look through in this reality are a bridge to your Self. There is nothing wrong with this ego, it's a wonderful mechanism that enables us to experience within this reality.
In order to make some more room within the mind for You, you'll first need to go through a process of disintegration. What I therefore would like to make clear is the manner in which you look at things.

Over the years we've seen all sorts of things, experienced, read and understood many things, at least that's what we thought. This is because there are three well liked games the ego likes to play; and if it can the whole day long:

- **labeling**
- **interpreting**
- **drawing conclusions**

The ego thinks it knows. That's why the window through which you look in awe at the world, closes. Everything you think you know better causes you to shut yourself off from the flow of life. Because once you come to a conclusion there's no room to sway with the flow; the flow which comes from a deeper level deployed by Self. At this level there's a natural discourse between all the connected energies. The direction you take is in the highest good of all, it's a natural flow where everyone's highest potential wants to come to light. A potential that your limited human mind cannot fathom. Everything always turns out different than you thought, because the ego is not programmed for unity, but for duality.

Do you want to step into the infinite mystery of life? Being your Self effortlessly? To live for the full 100%? To come to conscious Oneness? Then everything you think you know, will be punctured like a balloon pricked by a pin. For most ideas this would be an exciting challenge. But say for instance that we arrive on solid ground. Say for instance that you can't even be sure that the ground under your feet is real... or that you are a boy or a girl... or that the edge of the body you inhabit isn't the end of you?

Say for instance that everything you think you know is totally different than you thought. And the moment you think you begin to understand, it again totally changes. Nothing can be held down by labels, interpretations or conclusions because everything is continually in motion. Change is the only constant.

WHO AM I?

SOME QUESTIONS
ARE JUST MEANT AS
SIGNPOSTS
TO THE MYSTERY
WHERE ALL THE ANSWERS LIE
BUT WHERE NO DEFINITION
EVER SUFFICES

So I can't expect to know anything for certain, I can't see myself, I can only look from mySelf. But the question stays unanswered: then who on earth am I?
And that's why we're going to cover this at a deeper level. If your foundation gets shaken and you've never yet experienced what remains, then giving over to yourSelf can be very hazardous.

In 'spiritual' circles people often refer to the Love that we are, the happiness and peace that we are. This makes the image of ourSelf quite beautiful... *and* safe. It's not strange that we yearn for this. But Love is a word open to so many misinterpretations, because for most people Love sounds so nice. And we have all sorts of images about 'nice': gentle, soft, kind, compassionate... But this isn't what is meant by Love if you use it to define Who we truly are. Love is a word per definition that encompasses greatness but that what it refers to cannot be embodied in words. If we try and describe love with words I would use the following synonyms:

LOVE = LIFE SOURCE = GOD = REALITY = THE NOW = YOU

It is a limitless field,
an energy capacity that carries everything...

Wait a minute, you're saying that I am the same as God?

Yes. God is not an entity separate from us, it isn't an all-knowing being that determines you.
God is the life force in everything and in nothing, it is not a some-body. It's that component of energy out of which everything originates, every moment anew. It's that what remains when everything you identify with falls away. A 'non-identity'. Not a 'nobody', otherwise you'll be in danger of ignoring yourSelf as the source of life. You're not the personality you always thought you were, you are much, much bigger than that. The best way to explain this is with the following exercise.

Exercise:

Take a hand mirror or adjust a mirror so you can sit in front of it.

You're now going to look for yourSelf. Notice that this can be confusing.
Look at the mirror image of what you see as 'me'. If thoughts come up about the image, either positive or negative thoughts, let them go by, they're not important now.
Don't look at the face or the skin but now look in the eyes.
Look beyond the eyes, behind the pupils. Keep looking for as long as you needed.
Relax while you're looking. You don't have to find anything, there is no good or bad, look only behind the pupils.

Ask yourself (and say this out loud): "What am I?"
Watch out! You don't need to answer this question. The resonance created by these words will pull you deeper into 'seeing'. Ask yourself this question a couple of times to tune into it.
Let everything that arises come... and let it go again. Keep looking, without fixing on any conclusions. This is an experience.

It can be shocking what you see; the projections as well as the nothing. But that's part of it.
You may see the faces changing. That's normal. These are the convulsions of the ego coming to rest. Don't get caught up in these projections. If you encounter them then know that you have a choice. I can either believe in what I think I see (and what isn't good, nice, what needs to be different, what's scary or something familiar) or I can stay in not-knowing. In the space where the mystery unfolds.

Take a mirror and practice this in the next couple of days so that you can remind yourself Who you truly are.
—

Love, God, that what you truly are, is the only reality that is, in the here and now. The rest are projections. The reality lies deeper than what we can see on the surface. Moving out of the ego-mode and observing yourSelf is therefore being conscious of the real energy flow of the present moment. The mask of illusion will fall and the real You will appear.

HUMANITY

THIS 'NO-BODY'

YOU

EXPERIENCES
ITSELF
THROUGH A
HUMAN FORM

What you probably discovered in the exercise is that you're not findable. There is no 'you'. This can be shocking and disillusioning. That's why I swiftly want to look at the vehicle in which you house in this reality. Whether or not the 'me', this body, or this reality is an illusion we still experience. And there is a good reason for it. We made the choice to be here. So let's see the fun in it... And what's needed for you to feel free.

Effortlessly being yourSelf
begins with
total acceptance
of your humanity

Acceptance of the thoughts that pass by, of the feelings that move through you and last but not least of the character through which this personality fulfils its role in this world!

I might disappoint you with the following remark, but it could possibly also give some relief...

The blueprint which you have come here with
is hardcoded!
In other words: it is unchangeable!

All traits that you don't like about yourself are all part of the package. You can't change yourself, and... it's also not necessary. Because you are exactly okay the way you are. The only thing that can change is your perception of reality. But you'll have to live with your humanity.
It's not life that people struggle with, they struggle with the humanity, through which this world is experienced; with the thoughts, feelings and the body. Life is what it is. A small comfort: we're all taking part in this human experience.

Try and imagine that you let go of the discontent about this human vehicle you're in. You know that this jacket is not who you truly are and that it is the means to experience and serve this world. Rest in the knowledge that you are as you are. Trust that what you came here to experience you could only do through this body and this mind, with this character and that it's true. YOU chose this vehicle, on a deeper level, with subtle precision for reasons your limited thought framework cannot comprehend.

Undoubtedly you don't yet comprehend what's so special about this human manifestation, but resting in who you are is already a step in the right direction. It's giving up the resistance to what you don't want to be. It's all a matter of time until you see what's so special about yourself and therefore seeing what makes everyone special. What's so 'ordinary' about you is exactly what's so special and what moves so effortlessly. If you can accept yourself then all human traits will, through this non-judgment let go of their cramping up and come to light in their sincerest form. For example: the aggression you feel and you hate will, when accepted no longer come out forcefully but will find another way to manifest when it comes by. Strength, interest and passion, are all siblings of aggression. Don't forget that everything you repress will, sooner or later express itself in the outside world.

Accepting is however, not something you can just 'do', you can only 'non-do' it. Acceptation is releasing resistance, stepping out of identification with the 'me' which is no good and to relax in the position of observer. Being in connection with yourSelf and with all forms it expresses itself in: your character, life, and the encounters in it... The only thing needed is that you give up your resistance to what you don't want to be, to let everything that manifests in you and from you into your heart.

THE NOW HAS PRIORITY

**"WHEN YOU
CONTRADICT
REALITY
YOU WILL LOSE,
BUT ONLY ALWAYS"**

~ BYRON KATIE ~

The ego always wants to escape the Now. That's logical, because that what identifies, these thought bundles about who we are, can never exist in the Now. The ego dies in the Now.
And that's what we're most scared of. The paradox is that in the Now, You are born. Your real being, beyond the personality appears precisely in the Now. In the Now there are no worries, problems or fears because the 'little-me' that we thought we were and thought needed protection isn't there anymore. We have seen that the Now is the same as Love, as source; free of judgments. It is being in total acceptance with what IS.

JUDGMENTLESS – FREE OF JUDGMENT

CONCEPTLESS – FREE OF CONCEPTS

ANXIOUSLESS – FREE OF ANXIETY

TIMELESS – FREE OF TIME

FORMLESS – FREE OF FORM

CONDITIONLESS – FREE OF CONDITIONS

MEANINGLESS – FREE OF MEANING

TOTALLY FREE

You are free of every restriction or definition and this manifests through your body/mind.

I meet lots of people who want to live in the Now because there are no problems there, but they don't want to address their problems. They see the Now as a means not to have to deal with their problems, but they forget that everything wants to be 'seen' and experienced. The Now becomes a concept that will never fully be in the Now as the absolute Now is free of concept. We're running like a dog after its own tail, constantly running circles around ourselves. Truly surrendering is 'dying' to this moment and receiving *everything* that emerges in this *present moment* through you.
And I mean for 100% not just 99%. Only when you allow all sensations to be, will you go through the gateless gateway that is the Now. And

everything that lies on the surface at this moment then has priority. It makes no sense at all to look for pain that is still in your system from past situations or to put away the present emotion for later when you can look at it at your leisure.
The Now has priority! Always! If you try and go around it you are being unfaithful to the Now, unfaithful to yourSelf. If you contradict the reality (what IS) then you choose the road of suffering, it's that simple.

Do you feel like you want to defend yourself or are you tense, then you are still avoiding the Now, even if it's on a very subtle level. If you want to get somewhere or if you want to lose something then you will still not address what has priority. Everything in this moment which is present in your life, in the energy field as well as the physical world (which is an expression of this) wants to be observed by you. So, not in 5 minutes time, not in 2 seconds time, but Now. Because in connection with that Now you come into connection with yourSelf and you look from a viewpoint from which everything has already been accepted and your heart will open to what arises in your world. Free of judgment, free of worry, free of meaning...

Know that the only way to get there is by taking responsibility for everything that emerges through you in the present moment; in other words by fully saying YES to it.
You are the observer, everything can be observed through your Light and be transformed.

Take for instance the moment that you suddenly feel a dead weight is resting on you. You don't know why, or you already understand that stories are meaningless and you wave it away as not being important or unhandy. But the moment you wave away this sensation as 'non-welcome' you are once again running circles around yourSelf. You're looking from non-acceptance, even if it's very subtly.

The difference that I want to stress here is that not everything needs to be looked at or interpreted, but that everything may be, just as it IS. Waving something away is still 'doing' and being only an observer is 'non-doing'. Free of action. Whether they come through your head, your feelings or your body, sensations want to be observed, without You having to do anything with them. Observing through all the senses by which it is experienced.

So: stop expressing and repressing. Stop running from one illusion to another. Every Now, anew! You move your viewpoint from thinking and doing to feelingly observing, to experiencing through your six senses. You are receptive to everything that needs priority in this moment and suddenly time disappears. You are free of time. You merge with the Now. One with what IS.

FREE WILL

YOU ARE

AND

ALWAYS WERE

TOTALLY

FREE!

Your not feeling free was an illusion. All that time you limited yourself because you believed in all those rules and in all those concepts. The most obstructing concept of all was the 'you', you thought you were. But once you recognize this misconception then that 'you' is the most wonderful creation in this reality. Let's be honest... isn't it special that you can see colours! That you can hear sounds, taste and smell. And especially being able to feel... wow! What riches you will experience if you let yourself feel again. Do you feel the shift? Look around you. You can experience all of this because you have projected yourSelf as this person in an illusionary world! Wow! A world which is visible *because* we look through the eyes of this person, these glasses.

But who decides what happens in my life? Because I don't like everything equally. And if I had something to say about my life then I would have brought more happiness into it.
In order to explain this we'll make a list of all the motivations the ego has and the motivations You have for your journey in this reality, as there's a big difference between them.

To clarify this I will sketch the Self as an entity, even though it isn't. The motivations of the Self that I'm describing is the natural flow supported by consciousness, without labels such as good or bad, nice or not nice.

THE EGO	**THE SELF**
Wants more, better, bigger	***It creates***
Wants to feel safe and secure	***Is always in motion***
Wants to be someone	***Expresses what IS***
Wants balance and harmony	***Is here to experience polarity***
Wants to distinguish	***Knows that it is ONE and experiences diversity through this reality***
Only wants the positive	***Embraces the total scale of human experience***
Wants to possess and retain	***Flows freely***
Grabs to get	***Opens and receives while it's giving***

Let's look at the differences:

THE EGO	THE SELF
The ego is always busy	*The Self effortlessly goes with the flow*
For the ego it's important for its existence	*For the Self it's a game, and not important what the outcome is*
The ego does it mainly for itself	*The Self also, therefore subservient to the field of unity because it is everyone*
The ego wants to be someone to reinforce its identity	*For the Self it's about Self expression*

In short:

THE EGO WANTS

And it doesn't want... It especially doesn't want what IS and it wants what isn't...This may sound a bit funny, but imagine getting tangled up in this (like the most of us do). It creates a lot of agitation.
The shift we are making has nothing to do with the ego's will but that of Self. *It's all about the personal will dissolving.*
You may have discovered that you can be occupied by what you do and don't want but that every time it's a surprise what the outcome is, so do you have anything at all to say as person? And is the wanting of the ego not only just scaremongering?

Every form of 'wanting' puts you in unease. Wanting to interfere, to keep... to determine. It creates unease because we want to control. We want to control life. The past, the present and the future. And somewhere in a dark corner of our mind we know that this isn't going to happen, but secretly we hope that there are exceptions to the rule. The ego believes that there are exceptions and you follow. Please look at this mechanism carefully. Because it doesn't bring you what you seek. Only when you completely stop searching, only then will the journey find you! Only when you let go of wanting to achieve something, will it come to you.

You will only be happy if you surrender to the wishes of your Heart. When you as personality are in service of that what yourSelf wants to experience. Or, in other words to that what YOU wanted to experience through this person on this human journey. And in this you are completely free!

FREE, BUT NOT WANTING

Your freedom lies in the dimension of the Self and not on the level of the personality. The crux is...that you, as a personality have no idea what you've come here to do. You will only get a glimpse of this when you have stepped out of the ego-mode. So just realize that everything that happens in your life; that You have attracted it because you have good reason to. For a reason in the column on the right.

You may possibly encounter situations in your life in which the brain gets the better of you. It's busy thinking out choices. To the left- or to the right, according to what best suits who I am, how do I secure the 'me', my safety and my security? What if, then... But if you look closely at how choices are made, then you will see that the choices were already made before our brain started meddling with them. A choice doesn't get made by the ego, it arises before it becomes tangible on the mental level, on another level of yourSelf. Moreover, it has also been proven by quantum physics that action precedes thought.
You can deliberate, sleep badly or worry yourself silly, but you can also be awed by 'what will be decided' if 'you' don't interfere and if you therefore give it space to manifest through your human tools.
If you can take on a receptive attitude you'll see that your choices are 'inspired' exactly at the right moment you need to go in a particular direction (which can leave you in awe afterwards). You can probably count the moments in your life when you were surprised as 'I' could never have thought of that, but it went precisely as it should. Intuitions are another kettle of fish than trying to make a choice out of all the pros and cons you concocted. Intuitions can only penetrate through if you open up and relax.
If you're stuck in deliberating about choices you have to make then all it takes is one single moment of surrender, enabling the choice to arise inside you. You won't know when the decision makes itself apparent. You can't determine it.

PART II

YOUR RELATIONSHIP

WITH 'THE OTHER'

REFLECTIONS

BECAUSE WE CANNOT
EXPERIENCE OURSELF
WE HAVE CREATED
THE ILLUSION
OF 'THE OTHER'

We're now going to move from the relationship with ourSelf to the relationship we have with 'the other'. Because we can't experience ourSelf we have created the illusion of 'the other'. In order to experience a 'me' we need something or someone on the outside world who reflects the 'image of me'.
Dealing with yourSelf is one thing, however the whole integration process really starts when you make contact with 'the other'. The mental insight that you are not your body, not your thoughts or emotions but only the observer, has been understood and easily comprehended by many who sit alone on a mountain or whom immerse themselves in books all day. Most people will recognize the experience that the heart opens when the sun sinks beneath the sea. But truly *being* yourSelf in contact with the other...That's when we come face to face with the duality in ourselves. If you don't want to face this then you'll stay stuck in the process.

In the reality we live in every relationship is essentially dual. We experience duality in our contact with others because there is a 'me' and an 'other'. This is what we wanted because you can't experience yourself, you can only *be* yourself. An eye can see everything, except itself. That's why you experience yourself by means of the other. You experience your own dissatisfactions, your own playfulness, your own qualities and your own fears in interaction with another. It's through the other that you meet yourSelf. The way you move freely in respect to others can be measured by the level of freedom in which you live.

A lot of people who are developing their consciousness have discovered that the way we see the other, says something about ourself. They see something mirrored in the other. I would like to explain the difference between a mirror and a reflection.

What you see mirrored back from the outside world are your conscious and unconscious beliefs. You see your ego mirrored in the world around you. You see by means of your human jacket, your human glasses. The glasses are the ego. You look through the ego's glasses and see your own thoughts and emotions mirrored in the other. If you see sadness in someone's eyes then it's not unlikely that there's an uneasy feeling in your own stomach. If you get the feeling that someone's looking sternly at you, then the question is, how sternly do you look and act towards yourself, or do you think you deserve this severity. If you're tired, then

everyone around you seems to need extra sleep. The other literally mirrors your thoughts, emotions and body; your disposition. You can be conscious of what the other mirrors back, but usually the mirrors are about the unconscious beliefs acting out in your thoughts, emotions and in physical phenomena.
You see aggression in another because you have denied this shadow side within yourself. You feel irritation about someone who doesn't respect your boundaries because you don't make yourSelf visible, because you are unconsciously convinced that you have no right to exist. Everyone around you mirrors your conscious and unconscious beliefs about yourSelf and about life. You're good and bad; the good things which there should be more of and the bad things we would rather get rid of. So if you look at what gets mirrored back then you're looking from a mechanism that always wants to change something about that mirror. The level of the ego. Trying to change a mirror image is a bit foolish, because if you want to change the mirror image you will have to change the observer or the way in which it's observed... Wanting to change because of what gets mirrored back about your good and bad will make you unhappy. This is unsatisfying because you're trying to fight the symptoms and yourSelf just isn't complying with it.

I want to invite you to go further than these mirrors. Through the glasses you see with, you can be the observer of the mirrors you see. You can be conscious of all the projections in your belief system by looking at them without judgment, realizing that you are not these thoughts. The belief system is a pair of glasses from which you look, but it isn't You! You are the observer, the light, the source of all life and the other is a reflection of yourSelf.
That's because reflections reflect light! The other not only reflects your beliefs, but if you look from a different level they also reflect your light. If you look from this Light then you don't have to change anything about the reflection. Then you can admire this manifested light and enjoy it precisely as it is. And whether you look at mirrors or at reflections, they all appear *from* you.

- **mirrors** mirror your beliefs
- **reflections** reflect your Light

In order to see reflections you will have to step over the threshold. The threshold from ego to Self, through the gateless gateway. And once you start looking from this Self all beliefs will be transcended and mirror images will soften. They no longer need to be changed. What remains is solely your own stage. A stage in which pieces of consciousness and particles of Light play their game. A delicious play with you as the observer, the director *and* the player.

CONTROL

YOU CANNOT CONTROL
'THE OTHER'
THEREFORE, THE OTHER
IS ALWAYS AN UNSTABLE FACTOR

The Self dances with itSelf.
If you look through the eyes of your heart you can catch a glimpse of who you truly are as a reflection in the other. But you will also notice that once you take up your everyday life the ego will just keep carrying on where it started. This is because you're still stuck in automatic habitual patterns. As long as these patterns haven't let you go it will ask perseverance and alertness to recognize the ego in every moment, in every situation. The road back to yourSelf is, once again, the disintegration of illusions about who you thought you were. It's very tempting when interacting with someone else to switch on the automatic pilot, because here the automatic reflex operates in order to maintain and protect the identity.

We have already discovered that the Self dances with itSelf, however the illusion of the 'other' seems extremely real. And that's why it's important for the ego to control the 'me' and the story this 'me' stars in. It wants to determine:

WHO
WHAT
WHERE
WHEN
HOW

....how long, with what, why...the outside world must move, as it sees the other as ingredient to maintain its right to exist and to be a happy, living person. Children (who) need to prove through their behaviour (how) and their academic achievements (what) at school (where) that you are a good parent. The partner who (who) on Saturday evenings (when) has to set everything aside to give you a massage (what and how) so that you feel loved...
You might still believe that this is possible. Maybe you've discovered that you as a person, aren't able to determine very much and that you only sabotage what wants to unfold in its own time. But, oh... why didn't life turn out exactly as you wanted? That's because you as personality are not at the wheel, Self is! And the Self of the other. You are not able to determine who, where, when and how things develop. You cannot

control the other. The other is always an instable factor. You can't pin your safety and security on it. So don't even try to control the who, what, where, when or how. I know this tugs the rug from under your feet! But!

That's exactly where your joy is to be found! If you let Self determine, you open up to adventure and wonderment. It opens up paths which the limited mind never even dreamed of. By letting go of control, life can flow in full stream and be lived...and you will be surprised... and touched... really *be touched.*

You will notice that once you start seeing things from a different perspective that everything unfolded as yourSelf wanted...only at the time, you were not conscious of what you wanted (what IS), of who you truly are and what you have come here to do....and you tried controlling this by using the standards of a dualistic brain. You manipulated 'the other' to maintain the safety and security of the 'me', without understanding your connectedness as *one*. Whether you chase the illusions of the little me or not, we are all one consciousness and you are not in charge.

For someone who is still wholly identified with the body/mind, it's terrible to realize that everything always changes in this reality, that you know nothing for certain and that nothing can be controlled. For the person who has realized it, this encompasses the beauty of this existence. Because if you let go of the who, what, how and when everything will come together in your life precisely in the form that is most serving to you and gives you the most fulfilment.

Trust in yourSelf.

PLAYING ROLES

THE MANNER
IN WHICH THE EGO
TRIES TO CONTROL LIFE
AND ITS LIFE COMPANIONS

IS BY PLAYING
ROLES

Playing roles is a very important part in the process of awakening. Seeing through your own role play *is* awakening from a dream. Because the moment you see this, you step out of the clutches of the story and arrive in the position of observer. (Unless you once again step into the new story of: I shouldn't have played that role, I have to do it differently.) Let's zoom in on this.

We grow up and that what's so very unique about us gets squashed, because it's different, it shines brightly or isn't allowed. Be careful! Look out! Behave yourself! Do like everyone else, be normal! We all know these expressions. Therefore you learn to repress yourSelf and your unicity implodes. You start acting like someone you think the outside world wants to see and the tragedy is, that you often play a role which has turned 180° away from who Consciousness wanted to manifest through. This is how you hurt yourSelf. You deny your True nature. Why? Because we want our childlike needs met. We want to be loved! We want to be acknowledged. We want to be someone and get confirmation of this. We want to be someone who is nice and kind, because as a child we were seen and acknowledged when we were nice and kind. We want to be found loveable by the outside world, because we don't love ourselves anymore, we have become separated from ourSelf. This very basic need has nestled its way in since childhood and has, during our life become so mutated that we often don't even know that it's there anymore. Still, this is the most important reason on which the many roles we play are based. And that's the reason why we must ascend this need if we want to fully become ourSelf and if we want to grow in this awakening process. You're not free as long as you're still begging for the need to be comforted. You can't freely and effortlessly be yourSelf if you're playing roles to please the other for the purpose of your ego.

We don't only deny ourSelf because we want to be found to be nice and kind, all the ideas we have about life, who we represent and how we are safe therein, we think we need to protect. Our comfort zone. Our urge for safety and certainty about our personality.

I need enough money to be able to live and therefore I must work really hard, because I believe that's the way it works. I have to keep in contact with my family because that's what's expected, otherwise I'll be the black sheep and that doesn't rhyme with the image I have of myself, I have to keep on dieting otherwise I'll get too fat and no one will find me attractive anymore, at least, that's what I think, because I won't like myself anymore, I want to be someone who is beautiful and thin. I have to keep my front garden tidy, because I have to be sociable, because who 'I' am is sociable and that's how I want to present myself.

All of this is role playing in which we present someone who we truly are not. We do things in which we repress ourSelf. Unfaithful to our Heart. Unfaithful to this moment which is as it IS.

We play roles:

To fulfil our needs
(to be loved)
&
To protect our comfort zone
(to feel safe and obtain certainty)

We want and we protect ourselves, we grab and guard, we pull and push away... All based on the fear of the here and now because the ego bases itself on a big misconception: The here and now is not good. I am not good enough.

Once you awake from this dream and you see which roles you've been playing you may be shocked. You're living a life that is based on guarding your safety and certainty and which is equipped for someone completely different to who you really are. The real process begins where you wake up from the dream, out of the insincere roles you played.

"Being free is being self-reliant of confirmation from the outside world."

The biggest shock hits when you discover that you were chasing after an empty dream. You will never find safety and certainty in an ever changing world. And the need to be loved is a bottomless pit. It holds you a prisoner in a prison that doesn't exist. This is no longer needed.

Because the one you wanted to feed doesn't really exist. That 'you' is a thought and the real You is void of all needs.

But the ego has one more fundamental motivation to play roles and even subtler roles to uncover. Beneath every motivation the ego conjures up to avoid the here and now, is the fear of our own Light. The fear of the unknown, of that to which the 'me' must eventually surrender. The subtle roles we play we use:

To hide ourSelf

(scared of our own Light)

As soon as we enter a situation in which our naked Self becomes visible we hide ourSelf in roles and take on attitudes. We giggle, hide ourselves, fidget, change position and constantly draw circles around ourselves so as not to melt with our Light. The person opposite us also avoids true contact with the Self, if there is true contact he or she would also melt. We avoid vulnerability, but in fact vulnerability is the openness that lets Self shine through. The Self that is invulnerable; who you truly are is not vulnerable, it is only the image you have of yourself. What feels vulnerable is the nakedness, the openness and the authenticity. Yet this is where true fulfilment is found.

We're so afraid of our Real Self that we dim our shining; afraid of the enormous strength and greatness that will be released if we reveal ourSelf. The strength, the greatness and the unique manifestation that expresses itself in you feels so scary that we have all sorts of negative thoughts about it. Where we find the biggest rejection in ourSelf, that's where our greatest power lies.
Hiding ourSelf is repressing the intensity of life, but you are life. We repress the intensity of life by the attitudes we adopt and the roles we play.

This is based on a big misconception because essentially we only want to *be* ourSelf... being human. It's a continuous struggle between the inner urge to be and the idea that we're not good enough.
Once the role patterns which you use to hide yourSelf become visible, you create the possibility to step out of this.

Take the time to look at the roles you play and stay awake in every moment you are tempted to play a role. For instance when we are on holiday we feel freedom because we don't have to play any roles (of ourselves). That's also the reason why so many people feel trapped when they come back home, because we just pick up where we left off in our role patterns. Just take a look. Once you stop playing roles, you don't need to go on holiday because you come home to yourSelf.

DISMANTLING ROLES

A ROLE IS WHAT YOU DO

WHAT YOU ARE IS yourSELF

The process of dismantling the illusions we try and keep intact, has been set into motion.
But to let go of all the automatic role patterns we own is a bit too much to ask. So now you've been shocked about all the roles you play it's quite understandable that you want to get rid of them. Trying to get rid of something doesn't work, so be mild about it. Try and be mild towards yourSelf. You began playing those roles because you had good reason to. But it's time to see through what is visible right now. When you recognize that the role pattern has no purpose anymore, then it will let go of you on its own.

Maybe it makes you feel really scared to throw your roles overboard, who are you then, really? And therefore how should you act? It's no small thing when you suddenly become aware that the life you played was completely fake. That you're someone completely different than you thought you were. Not the nice, timid, docile girl but a strong woman who knows what she wants. Not the chivalrous, modest man but a real life leader...or maybe the other way around. Can you dare admit that you were much softer than this world asked of you? To see this and to be prepared to let the process you have stepped into take its course, will lead you to transformation.

When roles become visible during this process of awakening you will also go through a phase where you recognize that the roles you played were unnecessary. You will already be awake while playing a role, but the role will still get played out. That's normal. It's a twilight phase in which you're fully awake one minute and completely caught up in a dramatic role the next. At first you'll be in the role but once in a while flashes of clarity will manage to get through. Or you may be asleep for an hour and awake the next, going from one to the other. Or maybe you'll experience both at the same time; as the personality who plays the role (and ignoring the reality) and the observer who sees and realizes that it's unnecessary. At this point the role playing is starting to disintegrate. Try and be patient and present in this moment, it is only a phase. Not everything will be different all at once. Role patterns need time to disappear. Some stay because they don't hinder you to freely follow the Now.

It asks vigilance not to strand in automatic role patterns as a result of your being a slave to your beliefs about yourself and the world. The

thought that precedes is the key, the emotion is the warning signal. Be alert about thoughts and emotions such as: He doesn't like me; I have to comply to an image; I have to achieve something or else...Be conscious of these thoughts and the roles that are based on them, and you will have the choice to ignore the thought and to step out of your role. The minute you awaken, while in the middle of a role is a moment when time stops. For some people it's very tricky, because the ego doesn't want to step out of a pattern just like that, it had a good reason for it didn't it?
It is important to realise that you don't have to do anything right then, only surrender to the moment when time stops. This hole in time is the gateway to openness...but only if you dare to lose face and throw off the role; being vulnerable, open, and sincere. You don't have to be 'anybody'. If you step through this hole in time and you feel that your actions are in tune with the moment, and you leave space for the energy around you to move, then transformation is waiting for you.

When you step out of this mode your reactions will no longer be emotion driven (and thus belief driven) and you will no longer get caught up in automatic role patterns. Then the response you give comes from being solidly anchored in yourSelf; a response that is aligned to the here and now. A response that can move through you from yourSelf.

reaction → respons

This shift goes hand in hand with becoming a spiritually mature adult, (although your conditioning will still lurk in the shadows for a while, so once again, be mild towards yourSelf). Punishing yourself for a role you played just as you were discovering that it wasn't needed, is conjuring up a past that doesn't exist anymore. Every moment is new and you can never know how you will act beforehand.
The gift you receive when you awaken from being a prisoner of conditioned acting is the freedom to *be* yourSelf. Do you feel how a weight gets lifted? No longer putting yourself between a rock and a hard place to get what you want, to protect your comfort zone or to hide yourSelf. But *being* carefree. In awe of the adventure people call 'life'. That's when the mystery will touch you anew. It once again flows freely... from yourSelf.

STORY VERSUS SCRIPT

IF THE ROLES
YOU PLAYED
TO GUARD YOUR
SAFETY AND SECURITY
AND TO KEEP
THE ILLUSION OF 'YOU' INTACT
DISAPPEAR

THEN YOU'LL STILL
WANDER AROUND
IN THIS REALITY
AND STILL PLAY
A 'ROLE' IN THIS LIFE

What's all that about?
Let's therefore look at the difference between what I call a 'story' and a 'script'.

A **STORY** is what we make of something. *Imagine that... just like before...* A story forms in our thoughts and is always about then or later. A story is never set in the Now, and it doesn't cover the true reality. It originates from hope and fear and only plays off in our head.

A **SCRIPT** on the other hand is in fact life, the life you live in this reality, in this manifestation, in this personality... at this moment. A script is solely about the here and Now and is (without your judgment) solely what unfolds.

I call it script because when seen from the absolute it's a film in which you wander around in the 'role' you play. The 'role' you. What you really are expresses itself *via* this role. It's the role through which you wanted to experience and be of service to the united field of unity. You are both, the consciousness that shines through your manifestation, as the personality in the 'role' you fulfil. This is a completely different role to the roles you play to uphold your safety and security. It isn't a role to manipulate reality with, but a role to give expression to reality.

What it's about right now, in the process of awakening is that you

give up your identification to your role

However, you don't need to throw the 'role' you play overboard...

Let me clarify this.
If in your script you are the mum or dad of your children then Consciousness wants to express itself via you in the role of mum or dad. If you completely identify with this role then it will cost you a lot of energy to stay faithful to all your 'musts' and inner obligations. You're then faithful to your beliefs with respect to the role you identify yourself with.

When you no longer identify with this role but you do connect with it (and real connection can only take place in the here and now) then what you have with your children in this moment, is the role you have to play, as 'you', and not the role pattern. You will be astonished about the way your Self fulfils the role with you as its tool when you don't interfere (as a person) with who, what, where and when the role plays out.

You will notice that many roles are unnecessary and by just *being* yourSelf you fulfil a role in the lives of others. The role you are the most happy in, is the 'role' of YOU in whichever Now you find yourself, in whatever passes by in the script. You are the role YOU in all sorts of different connections and situations and that doesn't need a label!

THE ROLE OF THE VICTIM

REFUSE IT!

An important role to be conscious about is the role of the victim. Sometimes something comes by in your script and makes you feel like a victim. And where there's a victim role there's suffering!

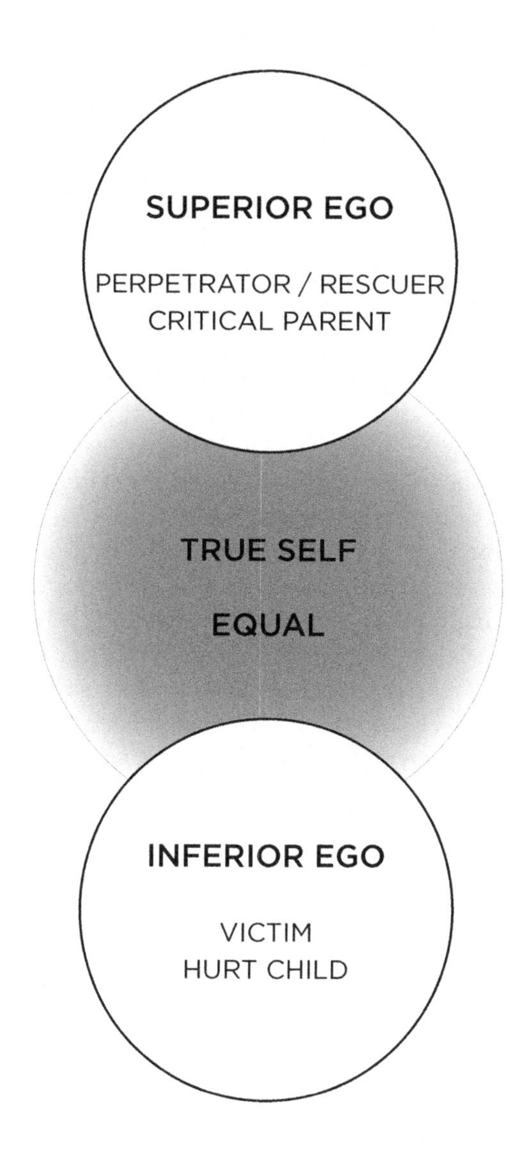

Let's therefore take a good look at what the victim role is really all about. The ego is responsible for experiencing duality. It's continuously comparing itself to others. It can either choose to place itself above the other or place itself in a subservient role towards the other.
In life situations it can also go two ways, either it tries to control what happens in life, or life befalls it.
It's either the master or the victim, superior or inferior.
The outside world, the other, is a projected setting in which this ego becomes visible. But in reality this only and solely takes place inside our head. The voices in our head, our 'my' mechanism are either superior or inferior to what happens, or inferior to the outside world. It jumps from one mode to the next.
This means it doesn't make sense to swap negative thoughts for positive ones, because you stay stuck in the ego mode. The way out of this mode is to disqualify both voices. To neutralize beliefs...and to rest in equality. There is nothing and no one more or less than you! There are absolutely no situations that befall you. That what the ego tries to uphold with these thoughts is not who you truly are. Everything arises from You and is within You.

The victim appears at moments of non-acceptance of life. We react either by trying to control or by running away from our Selves in 'I have to do something' or by taking on the passive victim role. The first method is actively escaping from the Now, the second is passivity. Grabbing, protecting. You can recognize the victim role when you pity yourself and there's a 'me' that something befalls. If you want to mature spiritually in conscious presence then you're asked to say 'no' to the voice of the pitiful ego. Know that a victim doesn't exist! Everything is an interaction of energy (action-reaction) between you and your projections.

OUR SHADOW

THERE ARE NO ENEMIES
JUST PIECES OF CONSCIOUSNESS
THAT VIBRATE
WHAT'S NOT YET
FREE
INSIDE
YOU

We meet ourselves when interacting with others.
And that's not always a lot of fun as our shadow also gets mirrored back at us. You never see the other, you always see yourself. What we don't like about the other is an unaccepted part of ourself.

When we get triggered by someone else or are in conflict with the other, then we're in conflict with our own belief system. When someone presses our buttons the chasm between our head and our heart gets exposed. Do you remember the figure on page 24? Once again we've landed in the twists of the superior or inferior ego.

The other has helped us to activate what isn't free in ourselves. He or she mirrors what holds you back from being who you really are; your shadow. Actually it's rather good news if someone irritates you, as in every irritation you openly meet, you're a step nearer to yourSelf. And then shadow can become light.

Take for instance when you find yourself getting really irritated because someone else takes over the conversation. It's an automatic response to react with anger towards the other person, but he/she is only complying with what we send out into the universal energy field. Do you really feel yourself worthwhile enough to be heard? Isn't it high time that you stop believing in this misconception about yourSelf by changing your view of yourself with 'I'm worthy'? No, because you're free of worth. Either you say something at that moment or not, it's not vitally important that you make yourself heard at that moment. It's all about you being free from your beliefs and if, in that moment it's your role to hear what wants to be spoken through you!

It will get even more burdensome if you can't forgive yourself and if you don't (yet) see that on a deeper level your Self thought this was the most functional situation for you. You want to take revenge as the other has done something terrible to you. Take a good look, who are you getting in the way of the most with these vengeful thoughts. The other? No, yourself! The victim becomes the vengeful perpetrator. The ego hops from inferior to superior. They are two sides of the same coin. Forgiveness is the only way to no longer being a prisoner suffering the duality of this coin.
However, forgiving is not something that you can *do*. You can only 'non-do' it. Forgiveness is the natural spontaneity of your true Self, as

nothing needs to be forgiven. So choose to no longer believe in the thoughts that precede. But allow the resistance that you feel towards the other to be. It wants to be completely allowed by you so that you can transform it in your light. Let the pain, the sadness, the disconnection to yourSelf just be, then the ego can settle down and you can once again connect with yourSelf. The Self where everything is already accepted and where the pain about deeds and vengeance can dissolve. If you want to completely be yourSelf then your heart will want to be free.

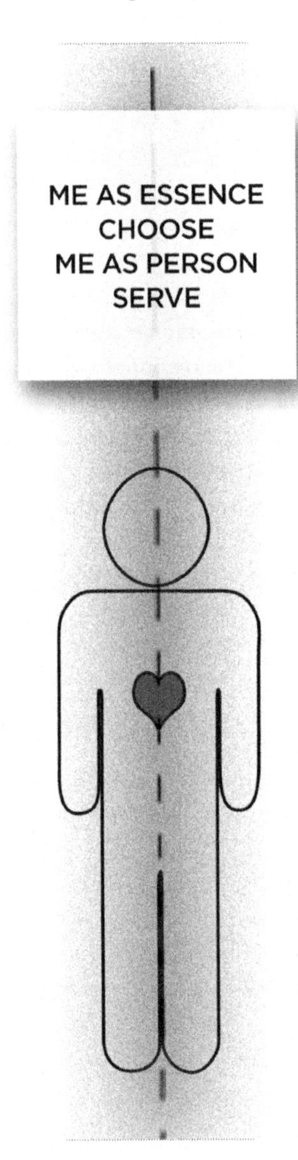

Turn your attention to the here and Now and know that on a deeper level all the experiences you've attracted for reasons your head doesn't understand are aligned to the motivation of the heart that wants to flow freely. Life creates situations to lead you to yourSelf. The stories behind the conflicts want to be seen through as being empty and therefore become neutral. Eventually your belief system will become transparent and all self-inflicted barriers will burn up in the fire of your Heart. Then there is a resting in not-knowing, and awe at how you as Essence, working together with the universe, carry and lead this personal manifestation.

And slowly the mind will expand, meaning it can align with who you are, and meaning what you wanted to experience via this human vessel can manifest in the world of form. The edges of your comfort zone dissolve...

This alignment can be a painful process because you no longer dwell in your comfort zone but are continually confronted with conflicts between your ego and Essence. Know that this is only ego pain. Give yourself the time and space that is needed to return back to yourSelf. Everything will appear at the right moment in your script, in service to your awakening. Embrace your resistance!

Exercise:

Take a photo of someone with whom you still have a bone to pick, such as your father, mother or ex-partner. Someone you still have an inner conflict with. If you don't have a photo then you can take the image of the person in your thoughts or look for a photo of him/her on the internet.
Now just look at this person in the photo. You will probably be confronted with resistance, vengeful thoughts, sadness, anger or disapproval...everything this person represents to you.
Maybe your head will fill with thoughts and memories about this person. Let them all go by. It asks a lot of powerful softness to let the thoughts be what they are, as thoughts can grab you. Even so, it's the challenge to let them be.
Allow all feelings just to be, while you keep looking at the photo. Keep on looking in the eyes of the other person and don't look at the face around it, as it will pull you into the world of form again. Keep looking at the eyes.
Maybe the face changes, maybe you'll even see yourself in it...
If you keep feeling violent sensations then you're probably encountering the fight you're putting up with your own ego.
Look at the resistance and realize that you have a choice; either to stay fighting or to surrender to yourSelf.
Are you prepared to give up fighting?
Are you prepared to bow to your Heart?
Allow everything that happens to just be, but stay out of the stories!
—

JUDGMENTS

WITH EVERY JUDGMENT
OF THE OTHER
WE SEPARATE OURSELVES
FROM WHOLENESS

When we return back to ourSelf we develop in alignment to the insights of Unity. This means that all dualistic misconceptions need to be made visible and be seen through. Our misconceptions are mirrored back to us by the 'other', as everything around you is you. The projections around you that you have not yet accepted, hamper you from being yourSelf. That's why in this lesson, we're going to take the resistance (in the form of judgments) as means to step through the gateless gateway. Your true Self is non-judgmental by nature, every judgment is a misconception about who you really are; we're going to pierce through these misconceptions.

'Judge not, and you will not be judged'. To stop judging is impossible if you don't understand what a judgment is. Judgments arise in your head as a much used pair of glasses we look through. The ego gives judgments about value on the basis of its ideas about good and bad. It's from our belief system that we look at the world and if something in the other conflicts with this then we experience it as a judgment. But please be mild about this. If you're not allowed to judge from yourSelf, then you place a non-acceptation on the non-acceptation... and that's not handy. A judgment is a defence mechanism to your own projection on the outside world. It can arise when you're with other people who trigger your 'shadow'. It can even be triggered by someone walking in the street, a colleague, a neighbour, a child, your partner..., they are all other copies of you. We point our finger at the other and therefore maintain our self-image. We would also love to tell the other what the truth is...our truth. But undoubtedly 'I have to be nice and kind' prevails over 'I know it better'. Or maybe we slip into an opening and give our self-image even more power by giving the other unasked advice... then the ego profits double up; it knows better *and* is nice and kind enough to 'help' the other. These are all mutations of the original non-acceptance in yourself. Every judgment about another is a judgment of ourself.

A judgment is also a lack of understanding about the roles each of us has to play, streamlined by the Self. I always assume that everyone makes the choices that are the best for them and therefore best for those around them. Accepting and being yourSelf is impossible if you don't accept the other exactly as he or she is. That's the way the cookie crumbles; the other is you. So:

Do you choose to be right

or

do you choose your happiness?

The ego gets uncovered when it gives up trying to be right. Or in other words if it sees through its own judgment as 'I don't know anything for sure'. It's at that moment the ego looks like a complete fool and that's absolutely awful for the ego. But a great gift to you as it asks surrender and everything is about this point of surrender. The death of ego. The moment the ego loses face. Because right there, in the openness of your true Self, Happiness is your state of being.

Catching yourself making a judgment is a chance to release the hot air and to melt into softness. To open your heart to the person you were judging. Then you see that there is total equality and it always has been between you. The enlarged ego judged, not you...

PARTNERSHIP

THE FAIRYTALE OF THE ULTIMATE RELATIONSHIP

Partnership is an important subject in this context as there are many illusions projected on it concerning the promise of happiness and a safe basis. When talking about the disintegration of illusions then relationships are *the* terrain to dismantle the ego.

From a early age we are told the story of the prince on the white horse who will give us a safe existence and the maiden who touches us with her love. We learn that we need someone else to make us feel safe and happy (and we all hold very colourful images of this).
When we get older we look for a potential candidate to share our life with. Then we can meet a beautiful girl who complies with the image we have of the ideal partner. That image was already clear. We think we know which properties are going to be responsible for our happiness. We have found a 'whom' and part of that is a 'how'. We fall in love and project all our conditions for happiness on this one person. Falling in love is making all our ideas and feelings about happiness, personal. As soon as we step into the boat together we begin by writing a manual about who our partner is and how our partner functions. A manual about ourselves to give to our partner so that he or she knows what is expected of them. On the other side of the manual we state our ideas about achieving happiness in love. (That'll be a complicated summary :)

So instead of trusting the flow of life and the projections (which arise because we have attracted them from deeper motives) we are busy satisfying our illusions by using our manual to manipulate the other. We want to determine how the other treats us and our life so as to give us happiness. We have lost this happiness, because we have lost the connection with ourSelf. The other has to save us from our unhappiness.

But, the thing you think will make you happy is exactly what prevents you from being happy.
We can spend twenty years moulding our partner to our needs and never achieve the result we want, or achieve our goal. Even then we will not experience the ultimate happiness we had expected. Why is that? Let me first dismantle an illusion...

The relationship with your partner is not meant to bring you happiness

True partnership is the crumbling away of all the thoughts and ideas hampering you to be who you really are (as you see all the non-accepted parts of yourself mirrored in the other). In this way your partner is a co-player in freeing the True You. The True Self that has always been happy because that's its nature.

The more your manual encompasses, the more you think you know what the other is or isn't, and how he/she will react... the more you drain the spontaneity from your relationship. In this way the partner has become the living 'image' we have of them... static... unchangeable.

Hopefully we will at some point open our eyes and start to discover that he or she will never give us what we were seeking. That this is what it is. You cannot change the other.
We can of course, go and look for a partner with a more fitting manual, however we can also welcome this script and become free in the relationship and discover the seed of our unhappiness instead of abandoning the projection of it. Otherwise in the next relationship you'll use your manual and start projecting all over again.

The more you search for happiness outside yourSelf in a partner (and therefore become disconnected from yourSelf) the more the other will mirror this disconnection.
It's so heart-breaking that the pain of losing the connection with yourSelf also gets projected onto your partner, sometimes even with hatred. Some couples experience pain, sadness and disappointment every time they look each other in the eyes. Because they look at all the pain from all the illusions and unfulfilled expectations that led them away from themselves and from the connection with their partner. Unconsciously (if you don't yet look from Unity and you're still prisoner to your emotions and thoughts), you will undoubtedly still feel hope, unfulfilled yearning, monotony, revenge, disapproval... unhappiness. Exactly the things you hoped your partner would save you from. However, the cracks in your relationship can open up the possibility of freedom. It's within your means to see that happiness is not outside you, but that you are happiness. Whereby a relationship can be transformed from a mutual dependence in satisfying each other's needs, to a loving connection in which happiness shines from yourSelf out to the other and increases. So, it's not from the outside-in (to you) but from you to the outside; because you overflow with an abundance of Love.

DESIRES

UNFULFILLED DESIRES
LEAD YOU TO
ONENESS

In the previous chapter we talked about how we make the other person responsible for our happiness.
We're now going to specify this in a certain desire, as it's usually something specific that you've elevated as goal for ultimate happiness. Including specific role patterns to make sure that your desire gets fulfilled. The paradox is, that you'll never get it because it just isn't possible. We humans react through our energy system. If you transmit yearning for instance (but are wanting recognition) then there's an energy flow to the outside which says: no recognition, no recognition. The other gives you exactly what you ask for!

But the ego sees this differently. When we're left behind, unfulfilled we feel a victim because of what we're missing and we point to a perpetrator who has caused this. We feel hurt by the perpetrator and protect and shut ourselves off for this person, from our partner. The person who should have fulfilled us, has become the perpetrator of our lack. And the big paradox in such a relationship is that the perpetrator also has to be our saviour. We're trapped in all three corners of the triangle; imprisoned between hope and desire. You want to be saved by someone you protect yourself from. What you see at work here is grabbing versus protecting. Attracting versus repelling.

The victim as well as the perpetrator as well as the saviour are a projected part of the unfulfilled desire in you. Everything you see happens within you. There is only You.
Let's take for example wanting recognition. The moment you feel you aren't getting recognition (such as a shoulder to cry on or whatever else you desire) you apparently have the feeling that you need this from the outside world. Do you totally recognize yourSelf? Do you make yourSelf visible? Can the other give you recognition if you transmit that you're not worth it enough to receive recognition? Or is the way you ask recognition not visible or not sincere?

If we go a step further: the desire that you're chasing after is an idea that you've turned into an ideal image. You feel the disconnection with yourSelf and think that recognition (what) from your partner (who) will fill the emptiness and thus, you stay stuck in this idea.
But you're chasing after an illusion because not only will you never get this from your partner, even if you would get it then it wouldn't fulfil you. You can ask yourself if the desire you're chasing after is really a desire

or has it become an obsession? And by a real desire I mean the wishes of the Heart which propel you further on your path. When you're with your partner you can be so focused on fulfilling that one desire (which is an idea) that very often it becomes an obsessive, insincere grabbing. An ego game that wittingly wants to get what it has in its mind, with all the intrigues that go with it.

There's a big difference between the desire to return back to yourSelf (the Self that pulls you inside) and the desire that we have made of it. We have generally interpreted and projected this lack of ourSelf on a specific desire (what) we want, to be answered by a specific person (who) at a specific time (when) and in a specific way (how). The desire of the heart has become a desire of the mind (control). It will therefore never give you what you seek. The happiness that is released when you are in connection with yourSelf and therefore with 'the other' can only be felt when you allow the victim, the perpetrator and saviour into your heart and see that they are all 'one'... Unity.

Try and feel this: What do you think you need?
How would you feel if this desire were satisfied?...
What would dissolve... and what would remain?...

Coming home in yourSelf.
Correct!
All desires remind you of the primal desire to return home and they show themselves outside you as projected parts of you.

So watch out for the moment you feel a desire arise and whether or not it is sincere; is it a recognition of the direction that your Self is whispering in your ear, or an immature wanting. A desire or a *seduction!* A seduction which wants to remind you to surrender to this moment.

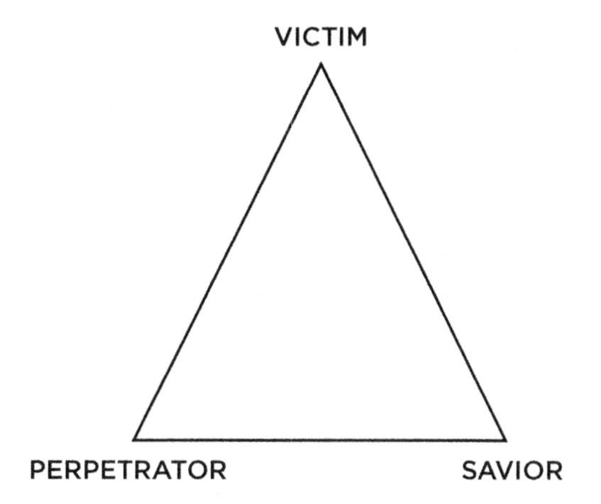
VICTIM
PERPETRATOR
SAVIOR

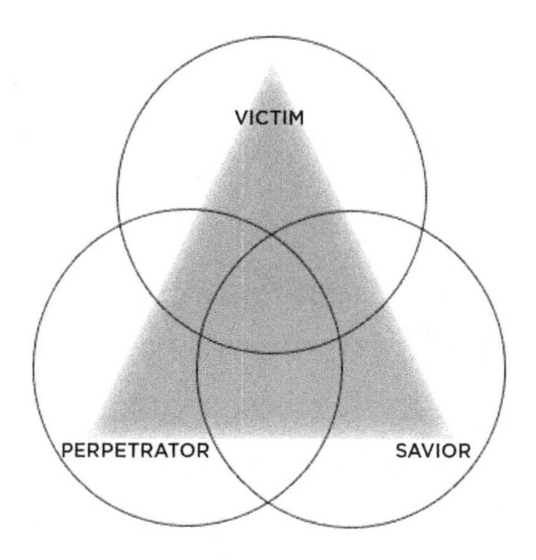
VICTIM
PERPETRATOR
SAVIOR

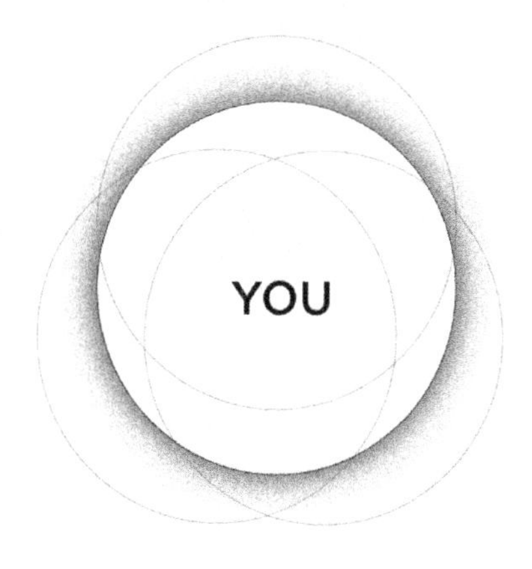
YOU

INEQUALITY

INEQUALITY
ONLY EXISTS IN THOSE
COMPARING THEIR OWN PROJECTIONS
WITH THEMSELVES
AND PASTING LABELS
OF MORE OR LESS
BETTER OR WORSE
THAN ME.

INSANE!

Seeking gratification for our desires turns us into a beggar and makes us per definition unequal to the other. Being in a dependent position makes freedom and being yourSelf impossible. Hopes and desires are power and manipulation techniques essential for the safety of the ego. This is not the case if you come from equality. Once you step out of the identification with the personality, over the threshold to Unity you'll see that we're all equal and that all the inequality you feel is an outgrowth of your projected thoughts and desires; such as the false idea 'I need you'.

I often see that one of the partners makes him or herself subordinate to the other. Often through false neediness but also purely because we have learned to do it so. Patterns carry on for generations! That doesn't mean that one person places him or herself above the other, they could have been pushed into it, as it is something inside you that keeps this pattern alive. But often you see that the other partner plays a role that fits the image of his or her ideal self, such as the' helper's' role. Or maybe even the role of the macho brute. If partners don't awaken to them, patterns will be kept alive by both parties.

I'm touching on this inequality because since the beginning of time we have been stuck in patterns in which the woman was subordinate to the man. (However this is not always the case, as I often see it's the other way around). The fact is, that for both partners it's a pattern that prevents you from living your full potential *as* yourSelf. In order to rise above this pattern you're being asked to be completely honest with yourSelf. Once you've recognized this pattern the process will have already started up and will quickly unfold.

The diagram on the next page makes this clear. What you see are the superior and inferior ego that cover the True Self. The lines which have been drawn are the communication lines. Not only in language but also in the energy... in behaviour... in body language. Everything reflects the position (superior or inferior) from which you look (and thus also what you feel and what you do) at the other. Are you looking from the all-knowing superior ego or from the needy victim? You might notice on checking this in yourself that it isn't always very clear. That's because the ego is unstable, it lives in a polarity and that's why you often jump from inferior to superior and vice versa.

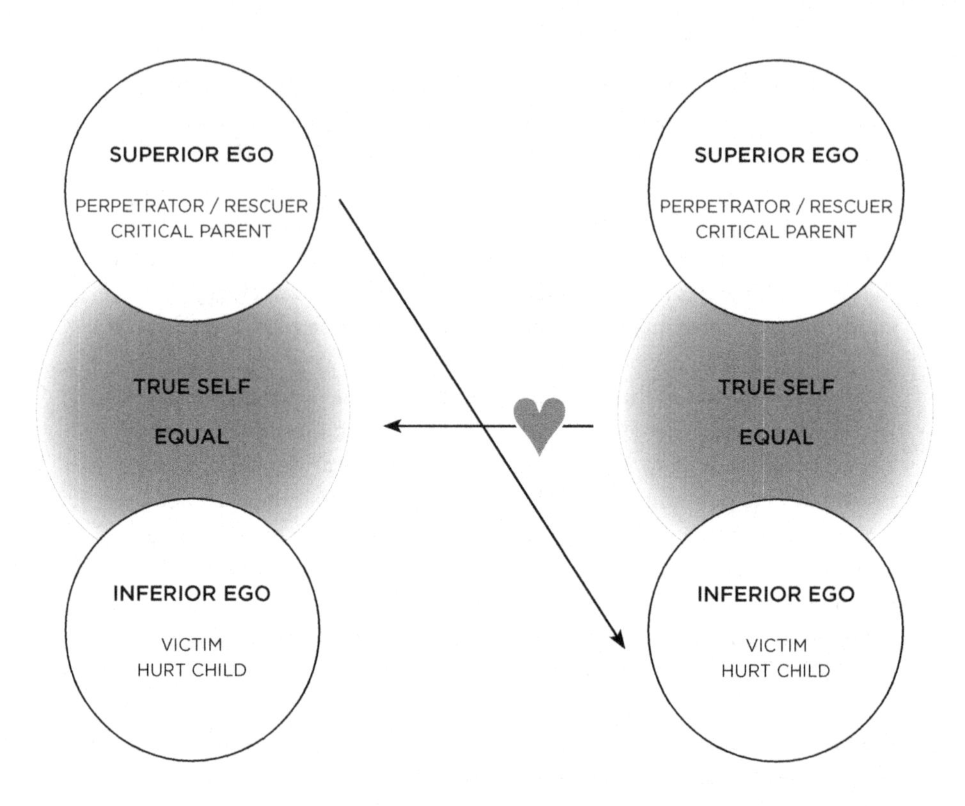

If you look from the inferior thought image then you automatically push the other into the dominant role (and the other way around). The one is not better than the other, they're simply two sides of the coin and both arise out of the ego that has no connection with itself, keeping its identity and therefore its safety intact. The inferior and superior ego want to keep a grip on you. You can investigate this; Do you speak from neediness, from false subordination or are you meek, and automatically docile even though all of this no longer fits?
Or are you coming from the I-know-better-for–you mode, do you see your partner as less than yourself... or do you feel the lesser one, but do you act as if you are better?

Do you have the feeling that you need the other or are you the one pushing the other away because you think you can do everything on your own?

All combinations are possible. What it's all about is that you become aware that you're trapped in the superior or inferior ego. Seeing this and admitting it will open a doorway to an equal connection. An opening to your true Self. Because if you can observe this you are no longer imprisoned by it! As long as you observe this (and are in the position of observer) this pattern can start to dissolve.
Once these patterns become apparent you often see people shooting off to the other side for a while, they start to kick the one who first helped them. Very logical of course, as it wants to become neutral. If one side of the coin has been repressed, denied and unaccepted, then the other side wants to be seen and accepted. Only then can it become neutral.

What I want to make clear is once you become aware that the game you've been playing was false, don't punish yourSelf for all the times you weren't aware of it. That's how it was and now it's different. You can no longer shut your eyes. Sometimes it feels like you're falling back into an old pattern. But deterioration is an illusion, it's not possible. It may be that something wants to be seen on a deeper level or that you need this experience for another reason; one about which you have no idea yet.

The equal and true Self is not out to win and not out to know better. If you are in an equal connection, one in which you dare to observe the other from complete nakedness you will see that:

Wanting to get → Willing to give

You are a vessel overflowing with Love. And love wants to express... and share. This gives a lot more satisfaction than trying to hold onto things around you in disconnection to yourSelf. It's catching. Everything you look at and touch with Love will be nurtured by love. And quickly, everything around you will breathe Love. Because what you transmit you shall receive. There is only You.

CONFLICTS

YOU DON'T HAVE
CONFLICTS
WITH ANOTHER PERSON,

YOU'RE ALWAYS
FIGHTING
WITH (PROJECTIONS OF)
YOURSELF

The friction that is sometimes apparent in a relationship has a purpose. Conflict is not always fun but it can be very meaningful, otherwise it wouldn't take place. Just like children in puberty or around the time of the terrible twos, there is a counterforce needed in order to become firmly anchored in your own Being. I've hit a nerve here, as the desires and the resulting distorted patterns we come across in our relationship are a legacy from our childhood. It's often about a maturation process in which we haven't yet come to maturity. Adulthood is about spiritual awakening and has little to do with age. Some people still react from childlike desires in their eighties without having much insight about essential life processes.

Don't be afraid of conflicts. They provide movement, rigid patterns loosen. On a subconscious level, conflicts can be attracted in order to lead you in the direction your waking mind cannot take. A lot of people are programmed to avoid conflicts, making concessions in detriment to themselves in order to avoid a conflict. Scared that their safety will be compromised. But when the propulsion back to yourSelf has become so strong, you will no longer be able to go around it.

Remember? All the anger and irritation you feel is a chance to look at what's not (yet) free. And that's what we want the most isn't it? Freedom? Your partner is the god or goddess in service of your awakening, in letting your true Self free.

Conflict is playing out beliefs which hold you a prisoner in duality with the other as team player.

Or the other way around. Apparently playing out beliefs in this material world is necessary because there is not yet clarity within yourSelf.

Be aware if the conflict started because the ego wanted to get its way or because it thinks it knows best or because you were being true to yourSelf and ego patterns between you are loosening up. In both cases it requires a certain alertness and you should avoid falling into the trap of living out your emotions. Fighting is always an ego-fight. The person who feels that the fight feels as a 'fight' is fighting with his/her own ego.

Or fighting with the ego of the other person, but that's the same. The other person is a projection of you and therefore you are always fighting yourself.

If a conflict arises and you're awake enough to feel the undercurrent of inner peace then you can't really call it a conflict anymore, but you'll experience it as a process. A process which probably needs you as team player. For whom or for what this process is conducive, you don't know... and you don't need to know. If there is insight needed then it will follow but it will most probably not reveal itself to you when you're in the middle of a 'fight'. So don't interfere with the result in that particular moment.

A lot of couples, but also parents, or friends all assume that it's very important to talk to each other when there's a conflict. I would, if there is not yet any insight, set the talking aside. Because if you want to put into language what you're experiencing it will first need to pass through the mind. The mind which is programmed to interpret and project. It all comes down to creating rules for improved relations with each other. That what has been loosened up by the conflict hasn't had time to ripen. Talking to each other from this stance will be superficial, dual and based on control. Everything you see has nothing to do with the other, only with your experience of the other, your experience, which is a projection of your beliefs. If you lay this on yourSelf or on someone else then you'll stay trapped in the ego game, in the 'story'. The communication lines will keep on transmitting from the superior to inferior ego and the other way around. Don't repeat it in your head or to your partner or to anybody.

Don't take the stories ego makes seriously and give every feeling the space to be without repressing or expressing it, then it can soften.

Sometimes conflict is still needed from the ego pattern, from identification. If one of you is awake enough to stay anchored in the Self you can help the other by lovingly embracing their anger or their grumbling without losing yourself in it. If you are awake enough about the pattern that is disintegrating then you might be aware that it's not necessary to battle with your partner, but that you can transform it within yourSelf. Everything depends on where you are in this process.

UNWRITTEN RULES

"YOU SHOULD NEVER HAVE THOUGHT UP THOSE RULES; THAT'S NOT WHAT LIFE'S ABOUT, YOU HAVING TO DO WHAT SOMEONE ELSE WANTS"

~ LUUK, 6 YEARS ~

Let's take a closer look at the difference between a relationship and a connection. No doubt you thought both were the same, but in reality they're much more of a contradiction than an extension of each other.

The connection is what we desire. A connection in love with someone else; where we can completely be our Self, in which we touch each other and strengthen who we really are, or a connection in which we hope to find ourselves through the other. To melt in unity, Oneness. And of course, these experiences are possible but it's a misconception to think it's because of the other that you merge together. In reality it's the other way around. As when you open yourself (for the other) or you surrender yourself in love making then what really happens is that you merge with yourSelf.
The relationship has 'claimed' this, as a relationship is a form, a concept of how two people should live together as partners. They agree on the rules about life and can therefore collaborate with each other. The moment you step into a relationship you sign a bunch of unwritten rules about how you should treat each other. It may seem safe but eventually it'll pull the plug on the relationship. Because these normal unwritten rules hold you back in living a spontaneous life. A list of these unwritten rules could look like this:

- You are 'my' partner and nobody else's. You're not allowed to look and especially not touch. You have to be faithful to each other.
- In everything you do you have to be considerate of the feelings of your partner. (Even if this means that you're unfaithful to yourSelf)
- The man brings home the income, the woman looks after the kids
- Every night you're on time for dinner, and we spend the weekends together.
- You have to please each other. ('how' is written in the manual!)
- You stay together until death do us part.
- In the relationship you share everything honestly, everything you do, think and feel.

Next to all these rules there are just as many expectations of each other. Some rules seem a bit outdated but don't forget that what our parents imprinted on us runs very deep and these rules won't be broken down very easily. And of course not everyone has the same ideas about relationships but we do expect that the other knows them, because

that's what the unwritten rules imply. I have never heard of people who make a list of rules the moment they decide to go through life together. These rules get played out in your head. And you expect that the other abides by the same rules. You can understand why these rules sabotage effortlessly being yourSelf.
Take for instance the last sentence. You have to share everything honestly. This is an internalized rule. You carry it inside you, the whole day. Your partner looks over your shoulder to see if you're complying with the rules. This is a rule that's interwoven with Christian ideas, mainly prevailing in Western countries. You learn at an early age that you have to behave and that you're accountable to your parents. And later to your partner. Or to a God who keeps tabs on you in a stern and predominant manner.

The most unwritten rules seem so obvious and normal that you don't even consider if they're the truth about life; living in freedom and unconditional love for each other. Is it really love when you hamper someone else in his/her freedom? Are these rules worth it, repressing the expression of yourSelf, your joy of life?
No, but unconditional love doesn't mix with fear of safety and security. That's the ego. Rules are only possible on the worldly level of form and as long as you live the connection from this level, you won't see a greater potential of a connection. Real connection is only possible on a formless level. And the world of form is subservient to this, not the other way around!
Truly living life begins when you step over the edges of your comfort zone... *in* connection with yourSelf and all people concerned. The Self is unconditional. And that's why a relationship is a contradiction to true connection. If this Now is a moment to connect with another person then it's spontaneous and not forced.

THE WE-ENERGY

A HUMAN
IS LIKE A DROP OF WATER

WHEN WATER DROPLETS
COME CLOSE TO EACH OTHER
THEY WANT TO MERGE

Making a true connection with each other requires that you open yourself. And the heart opens automatically when you let resistance go, when you stop trying to control, stop grabbing and protecting but start to look through the eyes of a child. By looking at the world from innocence, miracles will happen.
We're going to 'lift up' the connection with the other. Leaving the unwritten rules as they are. They had to be brought forward in order to be recognized so you can free yourself of them. We're not going to look at the why behind rules and patterns, we're going beyond that. The natural longing to connect and merge is a path that wants to be lived! Humans are like drops of water, when they come close to each other they want to merge. How the newly merged drop of water will move and therefore resonate within you both is dependent on what I call the 'we-energy'.

You as Essence have a certain energy tone, your own timbre and your own frequency. The Essence of your partner also has a completely unique timbre. When these energies merge together they become a 'we-energy'. A whole new ensemble. This connection has potential but doesn't say anything about you, or about the other...this is your 'we-energy'. When you live completely sincerely and you accept what IS and what isn't between you, then you can dance in full glory to this piece of music. A dance that nourishes and serves both your Essences. A form can develop in which the potential of your connection can bloom. Wherein you can admire and respect each other for who you are, and who the other is and wherein you recognize the nature of the connection in all its beauty. You will feel thankfulness because you know from a larger perspective that this is precisely what's needed.

The interaction of energy between you is to a certain extent very dynamic. You are different every moment and your partner is different every moment. But the energy tone and the timbre of your own Essence doesn't change. The nature of the connection and the 'we-energy' doesn't change either.

At this moment the major pitfall is the interference of the ego. What if what IS between you isn't what you hoped that it would be? Your 'we-energy' activates both of you, to actively put yourSelf in society, but you have an image of a romantic and relaxed relationship. Then you can do your best to feign this or to realize it, but the combination of your energies will activate you in that area. This can be very productive on a deeper level. When you want to change things then the question is if the form still fits the purpose of your connection. Maybe changing the form will succeed but you cannot change the connection. Because the energy connection always stays the same in whatever form you pour it into. Maybe the form is exactly the way it can best serve you and you only have to get rid of your ideas. In all new encounters there's an invitation not to let yourself be caught up in the relationship concept, but to let the most serving form for both yourSelves arise, on the base of which is the 'we-energy'. A form which is continually changing and which sometimes wants to re-form.

Don't get me wrong, every connection has a certain potential; the nature of the connection. This arises when you interact with each other, when you touch each other's energy field or make an energy connection from a distance. The interaction will awaken things inside you. Can you let go how it has to be, then there will always be someone in your surroundings who can serve what you need in order to bring your full potential to the surface. Then at exactly the right moments in your life your partner will be there when needed and you can let each other be free to develop, also with the help of others.

Completely accepting the connection that you have asks that you see where the potential lies and not want to make anything more of it than it IS (and honour it).
This is not only the case for the connection with your partner. In all connections, especially those that last for a long time there is a 'we-energy' serving both parties; which is the best possible piece of music you can dance to, the dance that comes from deeper layers in yourSelf and was the intention that you took with you when you entered this reality.
The interaction with 'the other' propels you forward on your path through the we-energy. From the momentum of this energy, manifestations in this world arise which you considered necessary for your development and expression. *Hallelujah!*

BREAKING TABOOS

WHERE TABOOS
NO LONGER PREVAIL
LIFE CAN FLOW FREELY

Being connected in freedom is being true to your own flow and respecting the flow of the other.
Sometimes you match each other in the flow but sometimes your partner is not the most suited energy to dance with in order to give your flow free passage. Then other people, other energy systems may come by who do resonate.
Being connected in freedom asks that you avoid the concept of a relationship, to move even deeper into the connection; to be prepared to experience everything that wants to be lived within the interaction. In this adventure you will encounter everything in yourSelf. As long as you both serve and nourish each other the connection will not (yet) be exhausted. Your individual development (both blooming apart from each other) can also be interesting and is something you can bring into your connection.

But it does ask openness to let go of all the security you projected on your partner. It also asks maturity from you as well as your partner to rise above the *temptations* of the ego. Because when you're in connection with someone you can't overlook this sort of tangled energy. Everything you undertake with other energy systems will also influence the connection.
Just note that there's a certain ambiguity in this: freedom versus egotistical behaviour. To 'acquire' the freedom to be yourSelf and to follow your own flow (longing) is not the same as chasing after the whims of the ego (temptation) and therefore reacting out of connection with your surroundings. Discovering freedom as your true nature and realizing that you are connected to everyone and everything means that you also realize that with every change of energy the whole field of Unity is set in motion!

So live the game of life from yourSelf, but in observance of the rules of this reality:

- **The one is everything and everything is ONE**
- **Everything is energy, what you transmit you attract and is of influence to all energies involved**
- **Everything is always in motion**

If you're ready to fully realize this, then it's time to break through taboos.

- **Everything has to be present in one person**

  We have already discussed that it's an illusion wanting to find everything in one partner. This is impossible and also not desirable. The human existence with all its possible experiences is endless in all its nuances. This belief really has to loosen if you want to live yourSelf fully. One of the ego traps is swaying to the other side by placing your wants and needs in another 'we' (if your partner doesn't have it then maybe your neighbour or colleague does). It's all about you following the flow of life, having faith in and knowing, that from a deeper level within yourSelf that you've attracted the experiences (in the right form and the right people) you wanted to live, so they can be manifested. You don't have to determine the 'what' or the 'who' you're only being asked to stay open for the 'what' and 'who' which the universe arranges for you.

- **Together**

  There are a lot of taboos on the word 'together'. When talking about a commitment, people often think that they have to do everything together. Sharing together, sleeping in the same bed together, knowing everything about each other, sharing every facet of life together etc. We determine that the form has to be together. But from a deeper level there is no Together. There is One, oneness in a dualistic reality. A world you move around in as You.
  In which a piece of consciousness wants to do justice as a complete You (not as a half of).
  The trap about 'together' is that you make concessions. Being unfaithful to yourSelf for the purpose of the other because of the idea 'together'. This isn't freedom. When you truly and sincerely follow the flow of your heart then the things that occur are in the best interest of all parties concerned.

- **Honesty**

  Being accountable is a theme we've already covered. This also wants to become completely free. You are responsible to yourself, not to the other. You'll notice when you research this taboo that the moment you think you are accountable or you have to conceal something (which is the other side of the coin) this happens when you are not OK about yourSelf, with what you feel and what you do. So don't use your partner to get permission for what you don't accept about yourself!

- **Sexuality**
  Certainly a book worth writing about, as there are many distorted ideas and repressed feelings in humans in this area. I'm just going to point to a few. Research your taboos on this. In what way do you look at the different roles in love making, does he/she have to be the seducer, and are you the follower? Does it have to be soft and nice or are you allowed to be rougher? What do you think is allowed and could be? Can you fully be yourSelf in lovemaking or do you reject yourSelf? Is sexuality only intended for an intimate relationship or is it allowed to live freely whether or not physically? Are you allowed to have feelings for someone of the same sex or even for someone else? Is sexuality something you're not allowed to talk about, is it dirty or do you see it as a gift of life? Creativity, following your passion, self-expression...these are all expressions of sexual energy. May this life energy flow freely?
  The disapproval on sexuality lies very deep, it is sickly and has, in many ways, smothered the seed of our life energy and is accountable for the most terrible, disturbed expressions in the outside world. (Yes, this needs a book at least).

It's important to realize that with all the taboos you throw overboard it's only really about you completely being yourSelf. Provocations or ending up in excesses because you're 'allowed' to can mean that you're passing yourSelf by.
So: always stay vigilant – every moment – and every situation!

THE MALE AND THE FEMALE UNIFIED

THE FUSION
BETWEEN THE MALE AND FEMALE
WILL RELEASE THE POWER
WHICH IS THE ORIGIN
OF ALL CREATION

When we speak of energy interactions then the game between the male and female energy is one I specifically want to mention. For many people this is what it's is all about in an intimate relationship (whether you have a heterosexual or homosexual connection) as the connection between the male and female is the basis of everything in this reality.
In connections between people, energy lines between them scan if there is an interesting, serving or nurturing game to be played out with this (new) contact. This unfolds by itself as energy flows where it can flow freely. It will seek out energies of a similar vibration (what you transmit you attract). When a male pole and a female pole have a similar energy frequency then these poles will merge, start flowing and activate each other. This activating of energy strengthens the spiritual light body. And light is the source of everything in life. A light body that is vital is the core of vitality.
You can understand how important this is. It would be a shame to pass by members of the opposite sex because you're in a relationship, as every polar energy with the same vibration works enormously invigorating. It doesn't matter if you, as a man are the male or female pole or are divided in 40/60 or the other way around. If you have the opposite energy then the merging of the plus and the minus of the battery will enliven and strengthen the energy.
In an intimate relationship the polarity between the male and female is the initiator in the passionate game of love. The physical act is an expression of what is being exchanged on the energy level. Everyone can agree that this gives life and makes you glow. Even without physical interaction if you open yourself to it, this energy exchange will take place. Sometimes this is even stronger than, for example, if you limit yourself to one-sided physical stimulation of the genitals, and therefore a strengthening of your light body.

I would even propose that the association with sexuality should be avoided in interactions where energies find each other, because sexuality encompasses an atmosphere of taboo and with our limited ideas about it we leave a tremendous source of nourishment along the wayside. We are tantric beings. We are a being that is built up of male and female energy, so it's very natural that these energies interact with each other... and what's even more valuable is the spiritual development. It would be a shame if by nature there is a nurturing interaction which you associate with unacceptable sexual feelings and you then subsequently break off the exchange.

Essentially every human is male and female, but these energies are not (yet) balanced. In many ways the masculine (ego) has prevailed and the feminine (heart) has been forgotten. This also applies to women! Returning back to yourSelf is about surrendering the masculine to the feminine so that they come together and merge in the Source of origin. The all-encompassing Consciousness... You.

When the ego surrenders to the heart, you move from the horizontal line of the past and future to the now (Self). Just like this symbol so beautifully implies, life awakens on the border of being and not-being. The circle in the middle gives an indication of this. The merging of the male and female as One. This is a movement that wants to unfold *in* you and subsequently in the intimate connection. As truly merging with each other can only take place when the ego has surrendered to the heart in *both* people.

Through the balance between the male and female in ourSelf the world around us will also change. For years, woman and therefore the symbol of the female heart has been repressed and not taken seriously, letting the ego get the overhand.
But Father Consciousness has also been forgotten or been poured into false images.
The shift from an ego-led being to a heart-led being; in which we as humans now find ourselves, will place the ego in its serving function once again and the heart in its leading function. This begins with the realization that there is a full cooperation between the male and female. Neither of the two want to be repressed, they only want to be balanced once again. And God wants to be seen for what it really is, the driving force of the yin and yang.

PART III

YOUR RELATIONSHIP

WITH YOUR PHYSICAL BODY AND THE MANIFEST

THE SPIRAL OF CONSCIOUSNESS

LIGHT ART THOU
AND LIGHT
SHALT THOU RETURN

The male and female principle is the nature of this reality.
Once we were only Light. This light broke up in polarities of light particles; male light particles in various colours and female light particles in just as many colours. And as you already know when you bring all colours together, which colour do you get? White Light. Everything together is nothingness.

Nothing and everything all at once, that's what we are!

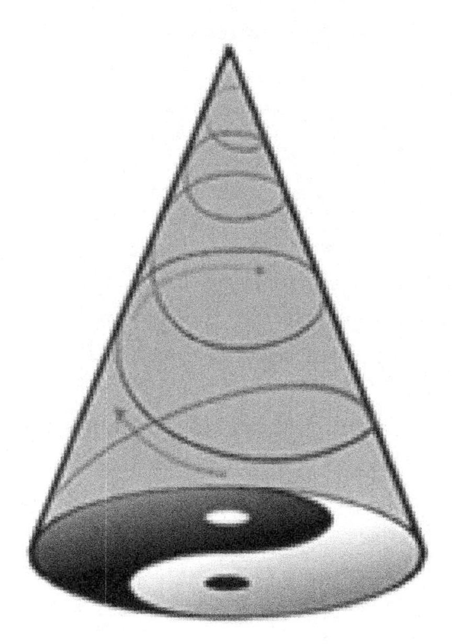

This reality, the world of form is an orchestra of polarities. Our awareness takes place on the podium of this earthly plane. The polarities are in total harmony with each other, even so most people only want to identify with the light aspect and have a lot of resistance for the darker aspect. That's why we experience this world from duality and therefore the Oneness, the non-duality which everything has originated from is forgotten.
We experience these significant differences and the non-acceptation between dark and light in ourselves, in the other and as reflection in the world outside. In the diagram on the previous page you can see a cone with the yin-yang symbol at the base; the male and female pole. The framework around the yin-yang symbol is characteristic for the reality we live in. It's a symbol for the finiteness of everything. The framework of polarities is where we experience our being human.

This book, as I have mentioned earlier, is divided into four main categories in order to give a complete and sound image of the shift we are all going through. All these aspects and sub aspects move around at the base of the cone.

It's all about:

- **Your relationship to yourself**
- **Your relationship to the other**
- **Your relationship to your physical body and the manifest** (I'll explain this further on)
- **Your relationship to your service to the field of Unity.**

Cyclically and in a spiralling manner we are challenged by life to bring consciousness into all aspects in order to realize the endlessness of our true Self. This is the point above the cone. This is the point where you awaken out of the dream, fully awakened. The first 2 aspects have already been discussed. Now we're going to make a start on the physical reality in which we live; the manifest.

We experience and go through certain themes we encounter in all these aspects. The cyclic nature makes that these aspects continually return, wanting to be experienced at an even more subtle level every time. In this way you penetrate further into the core of your being, your true Self, which is in the absolute centre of all these cycles. We recognize the formlessness in the world of form, and eventually from the formlessness we can experience the world of form. This is the shift that is now occurring. Firstly returning back to yourSelf and stepping out of the story. And then experiencing yourSelf as form *in* this reality. The nearer you come to your natural state of being, the more the ego will subside and the more transparent you'll become with respect to the polarities, the freer you are to be yourSelf.

This spiralling development is the natural way to transformation. It is the traction of your Essence to freedom, to the centre of who you are. Every facet of life influences all other facets. If you have a physical ailment you will also find problems in the relationship with yourSelf and with the other. It's the norm that you first need insight about themes at the bottom of the cone before you can continue your creative process. If you are not okay with the world and you can't look after yourself then you're not yet ready to make the transition within the spiral to the next level above. You will slide back down the spiral of consciousness. A lot of people who are into the world of 'spirituality' might feel resistance to this 'earthly' perspective (do you see the duality in this?). It's amazing to see that as soon as the term 'spirituality' comes up, looking after yourself and making an income doesn't match and the earthly world becomes inferior. Without the acceptation and the managing of this, the Self cannot fully shine in this manifestation. That's why in the following chapters we will pay particular attention to the physical aspect of being human and this earthly reality.

THE PHYSICAL BODY

OUR BODY
IS THE VEHICLE
WITH WHICH
WE CAN EXPERIENCE
THIS WONDERFUL WORLD

You have already discovered that the journey back to yourSelf is all about the crumbling down of what you are not. In other words, with the identification to this. Sometimes I get asked if we have to let go of the physical body in order to surrender to our Self. This feels very unnatural because the body is the vessel by which you experience yourSelf in this reality. The body is your physical manifestation. So there's no need to let go of it. It's only really about your *readiness* to lose everything, but it doesn't mean that this is going to happen. Even more so, I'd like to turn it around; connect fully with your physical body. What it's about is you letting go of your identification to it.

Note as a guidance to everything you encounter in life:

Connect fully to it
but don't identify with it

Connecting to your body is embracing and accepting it in its entirety. All your non-acceptations want to be allowed in your heart; non-acceptation of your form, your state of being and your limitations. A lot of people don't have a very good connection to their body. They don't pick up on its signals and neglect it due to lack of a real connection with it. The body is a very special vessel. Try and imagine how it has built itself up all these years, how it has formed and manifested on an energetic level, precisely aligned with who you are, because:

Your perception forms your physical body

Disapproving of your physical body is therefore disapproving of who you are in totality.

As we have seen of your disapproval of people around you, disapproving of your body or a part of your body is non acceptance as a result of a belief about yourSelf. If this body doesn't match with how you feel, then there's probably a gap between your belief system and who you truly are (as in the diagram at page 24). Every part of your body is built up from what you transmit in energy, based on your conscious and unconscious beliefs.

If we take a closer look then the body is a projection of light, of energy particles and photons, which builds itself every moment anew on the basis of your total being. The physical body is a divine hologram and every moment you are completely new. We think we know our reflection but the image we have of our body is not fixed. What you find and think of your body doesn't exist anymore.
Let the identification with this fixed image go, then you can be amazed about this mysterious object with which and through which we experience this mysterious world. It is not who you are, it is a temporary vessel.

WE ARE NOT SUPERIOR
TO NATURE
WE ARE NATURE!

AND WE WILL NOURISH OUR BODY
WITH THE SAME INGREDIENTS
AS WE CAME INTO SUBSTANCE WITH

Is food important when talking about effortlessly being yourSelf?
No, but your relation to food is! Some people have real issues with food. Beliefs hinder how relaxed we eat and how able we are in extracting enough nutrition from our food. Your body really does demand care and attention. There are few people who can live off light. Our current level of (collective) consciousness is simply not ready for this. Let me make a list of how unhealthy our relation with food is:

- Overeating to repress stress and anxiety
- Not allowing yourself to eat because you might gain weight and are therefore no longer desirable
- Eating super healthy foods out of fear for food we label as 'unhealthy'
- Unconsciously eating because of the disconnection with your body (then food is no longer food)

What I miss in relation to food is that the food you eat, in *this* present moment is aligned with your energy system and how you feel. So: eat consciously and with feeling.

Choose food of the same energy frequency as yourself, in this moment.

You don't have to physically touch all types of food as there is no space in energy. By only thinking and simultaneously focussing on the energy level of a nutrient you can feel if it is aligned with what you need in this moment.
Maybe you need the light freshness of a pear or the grounding density of meat for instance, (however for some people with a subtle energy field this will be too heavy).
On the internet I found a photo of the energy emission of a mushroom. Of an organic and a treated variant; the organic variant has a much stronger and less distorted emission. It relays that food also has an energetic value and that there's a big difference between food types and ways of cultivating. I'm not cheering on using exclusively organic food, although I do prefer this myself.
Just don't get trapped in the pitfalls and become obsessive. When you do your shopping feel! And don't think! Look what attracts your

attention, what makes you feel happy? These are good markers. Do you feel that it nourishes you or do you feel washed out? Maybe you'll find what I have to say a bit strange, or maybe you'll feel the excitement of the child in you: completely happy just by seeing all the beautiful colours in the super market and only wanting to smell, touch and taste. Go and experience this! Enjoy instead of making it a 'must'.

A lot of people are not conscious when they're consuming food. This has nothing to do with the sort of food you eat. Take for instance when you eat chips, sometimes you greedily gobble them up all at once without really feeling nourished or feeling how they align with what your energy system needs in this moment. *Being* conscious and continually connected with the Now also asks continual awareness for the changes in the Now and moving with these changes. So do stop if your plate is only half empty because it's ok to do so.

No, this has nothing to do with Self-realisation, but once you see how this reality works, you will work with the natural laws instead of going against them (like rowing against the stream). Going with the flow is being conscious; always and everywhere conscious of the flow and being completely aligned to it.

If you are completely conscious that your body is You, an extension of you, then you will handle this wonderful projection and everything it is connected with in a different way.
You are not your body, but your body is you!

SICKNESS AND PHYSICAL HANDICAPS

**"MUMMY,
MY TUMMY SAYS
THAT I HAVE TO LIE DOWN."**

~ MEES, 4 YEARS ~

Cells in your body are being guided by energy and the energy is led by your focus. You don't even think about most parts of your body because you take them for granted. Your body has arms and legs, your cells form these every moment, as a cemented 'belief'. This belief has nestled into the cell memory of your body.

Sicknesses are a result of a disruption in the natural energy flow expressing itself in the body. It is a 'degeneration' of certain cells, determined by your conscious and unconscious focus. The cells in your body do exactly what are asked of them. Don't see it as something that's wrong if the cells don't work together with others because you give them mixed signals. One side wants to express itself and the other side wants to repress... two directions, two different ways in which cells form based on opposite energy frequencies. The natural side is self-expression and the opposite direction is ignoring yourself, which arises from the belief that you are not good enough or that something isn't right. This unnatural energy-cramping guides cells within your body making them move in an unnatural direction.

When you don't listen to the Self; to the energy in this moment it's an attempt to turn the flow of the river the other way around. In every moment the energy balance subtly lets you know what is needed. It wants to stay in its natural balance. That's why you get sleepy, you feel hunger, feel the impulse to go to the forest, feel you don't want to be in a place where the energy doesn't feel good for you, or get an ominous feeling if you let yourSelf down. If you ignore these signals your system will become unbalanced and will develop sickness as a regulator.

What we call sickness and label as 'awful' is purely and only the manifestation within the body of a certain energy frequency. The body is an enormous creation that fully works together with all the layers of yourself. It is a loyal servant that tells you precisely where there's rejection and therefore repression of yourself. As long as you don't resist this here and Now and how it wants to flow through you, then the body will reflect its divine origin.

To be totally clear, what we're talking about here is what happens at the base of the energy. This is important because the effects in the body express themselves with a built-in delay factor. So, turned around, looking for remedies in the material reality will also be

delayed. The base of all imbalance is found in the energy and it takes place on vibrational levels. When we look at a person as a body with thoughts and emotions and we translate this into energy, then all these components will vibrate at a certain frequency. Our thoughts vibrate very subtly, so subtly that we almost don't notice them. When we take our thoughts seriously, and we believe in them, the thought vibration takes leave to vibrate in the emotional body, which is a bit denser in structure and easily visible for most people. A lot of people ignore these vibrations, if this happens the vibrations will only become stronger. Because they're being ignored, they're not able to be transformed in a natural way. They're hampered and keep trying to follow their programmed flow. If this isn't possible then the blockage will get even bigger, like a lock door which closes in water. The water level will then rise and press even harder on the lock doors and try and find alternative ways to keep flowing because this natural movement never stands still. As the power of the frequency increases and alongside the natural flow of the body an even greater flow is initiated, it will bring movement in physical cells and will express itself in the body, for instance, in an illness. If you feel like a victim then you'll give even more attention to it and the process of degeneration will only quicken. The key is always *acceptance*, before any change can take place.
Approach this physical expression or 'sickness' with mildness. Stress, which has been accepted as the most important cause of sickness, is nothing more than structural resistance to the present moment and ignoring your own signals.

When the body is 'ill': when there are two counteracting energy streams active in the body, then the only thing that is needed is that they once again flow in their natural direction. Sickness or tiredness is an invitation to re-establish the connection with your true nature. When you're truly yourself and you give expression to yourSelf, a great part of the unnatural flow will be lifted as you're no longer unfaithful to your Essence. Then the lock will open and the natural flow will be re-established so that all counter frequencies comply with this powerful energy.
This being faithful to yourSelf again is not something you can do, but something that will naturally flow if you stop doing... stop repressing... stop resisting what IS.
Then the energy flow will turn around so that the 'wrong' cells stop

propagating in your body. Changing the direction of energy is somewhat similar to a lock being opened, filled with healing water, the lock of your natural flow. As soon as you stand up, give yourself freedom, and you spread your arms the lock will open with your natural flow and the countering flow will be overpowered and taken along with it.

If we talk about congenital diseases and disorders then we're talking about life circumstances: the film screen in which you experience life. There is nothing wrong with such a sickness. Let go that you have to be cured, embrace only what your faithful servant gives you. It's possible that your being human wanted to express itself through a handicapped body (which was the most suited setting concerning what you came here to do).
A beautiful example of this is the boy Niek Zervaas who had multiple disabilities and whom they thought was also mentally handicapped. Until his 18th birthday he couldn't move, not even his facial muscles. Then he learned, by using a letter board to communicate and turned out to be a very intelligent, free spirit. For years he spoke about love and breaking free of your mental limitations. He was able to observe, purely because he never had to take part in matters of the mind, upbringing or education so he remained pure. He explained that as Consciousness he wanted to experience himself and therefore chose a body with a handicap and epilepsy.
This offered him many experiences *and* possibilities which would otherwise have been unheard of. So, there doesn't necessarily have to be a blockage with sickness, but the scene you find yourself in will always support the return back to yourself.
Whatever form it takes... embrace it! Connect with it but don't identify with it!

MATTER

**"MUMMY,
IN MY NEXT LIFE
I DON'T WANT
MUCH STUFF ANYMORE,
IT MAKES ME RESTLESS"**

~ LUUK, 6 YEARS ~

Everything is energy, thoughts, feelings and matter. Matter is the most dense, physical form of energy, but there are differences within it. The energy of a block of ice vibrates less quickly and the atoms are further apart than in streaming water. In that case it's not all that strange, in a society which is so ego-led that matter has taken on the tone of the ego, with its consumption industry, greed and depletion of the earth's resources. A lot of people greedily welcome the consumption society, others feel increasing resistance towards it. This resistance is logical once you see that the cause of the misery is the imbalance between the head and the heart... But even so, change is only possible when you face these issues exactly as they are.

Matter isn't a problem and is needed for our primary necessities. Luxury, ease and technical aids can also be helpful to humans. Matter is also creation. But it's the way we relate to matter that lets us see how free we are or if we're in the grip of the ego. The ego can also be seen as synonymous to the will, and when the will is at the wheel unrest will prevail: 'wanting to have' in this case.
Matter is a much loved terrain where the ego can gratify itself. It looks for fulfilment in things and its identity in possessing things. We all know this. In the last 10 years it was very normal if you wanted something you just bought it. But you had no idea how much agitation this created within your inner world and how it distorted the balance between the male and female in yourSelf and in mother earth.
Go back to a moment in time when you really wanted something. Do you remember such a moment? Were you dreaming about wanting something, your heart (correction; head) made a leap of joy and suddenly the moment arrived when you could buy it and you were eternally happy? You weren't happy because you got what you wanted, but because *for a moment you wanted nothing*. You were:

FREE OF WILL

Sometimes that joy and the peaceful contentedness stays a while, a month, a week or sometimes a few minutes. Then suddenly the ego wants something else and the agitation of wanting grabs you by the throat again. So try and see that getting something makes you happy but being free of willing, transcending the ego is being freed from the will.

I remember a family party where my nephews and nieces showed each other their iPods, iPads and iPhones. I leaned forward to admire these new gadgets (as I'm really fond of all sorts of apparatus) but I hadn't bought any in years because of a company bankruptcy.
I was taken in by greed, if only for a moment, 'I want it too'! Immediately I felt great unease, but luckily I recognised it as a result of a disconnecting thought and I stayed out of it. I then realised how detached I had become to things and how much inner peace this had given me. I felt so rich!
I'm not saying that it's wrong to enjoy the luxuries of life. Enjoy luxury if you can afford it and if you are sound in your purchase. But watch out! When wanting has you in its power you're a prisoner of your own greed *and* of your fear of losing it, because the more things you need for your identity or wellbeing the more your fear arises in losing it.
In this era the abundance of material things has imprisoned people. Houses are too small, you have to tidy up your things, store them, clean and maintain them.
Time which could be using to follow your passion (which I will cover more fully further on in this book).
If you want to be freed from the grip of the ego, then you'll have to detach; and in this case detach from matter. The crisis we're now all facing is for some of us, a blessing in disguise. The natural purification of something that has become totally imbalanced. How would you feel if you were to ride around in a shabby second hand car? Do you dare buy your clothes in a second hand shop? Do you feel better or worse than people who need financial assistance? When there is no money to buy a present for someone's birthday, can you tune into your own creativity? Could you be happy with yourself if there were no things to attract your attention in this moment?

A much healthier attitude to matter (the material world) is in truly seeing it for what it is. If you look at an object through the eyes of your heart then you will see that it has no worth. It doesn't need an interpretation and you therefore look beyond the level of the ego. It then becomes evident is that this object is only being supported by mind-power. Without this energetic support it wouldn't exist. If you look at it from this perspective all matter is to be honoured without needing it for your own safety or status. That's when matter can become a reflection of our *being* conscious. Creation stays, that's the great thing about this reality. No doubt there are other ways of producing matter

and material things but more in connection with as respect for all the engaged energy's during this process. Other products will come onto the market serving the humans who live from their inner guidance, and products serving the ego will lose their attractiveness.
You are the key to all this, everything begins at the mid-point where everything originates and that is you. Are you connected to yourself and therefore with everything you come into contact with? Is the matter that you now have surrounding you aligned as a living expression of what you are?

MONEY AS THE BASE OF SECURITY

THE MOMENT
YOU STOP
GRABBING AND PROTECTING
ABUNDANCE
WILL BE YOURS

An even more fundamental fear we encounter concerns money, as money is needed to supply us with our basic needs such as food and housing. This is not only the case for people with a minimum income, but also and maybe even more so for people with a lot of money (as they often have a greater fear of losing it). There are people who are filthy rich who can't sleep at night because they're constantly busy trying to keep their money safe. So if you're worried about not having enough or you have too much and fear losing it, it's all the same. Money is loved and hated in this world. Money drives us, it is our slave driver. The monetary system hampers many people from being who they are and from following their passion, it keeps humanity limited within old patterns.

Money was originally intended as a way to bargain or barter but has in centuries past become seriously clouded with lust for power and greed. When money regains its 'honest' intention we will all be a step nearer to a sincere life in alignment with the deeper layers of ourSelf. Whether humans are willing is the question, and if we can turn back even more so. It's much more plausible that a whole new system will arise with a clear intention or a radical insight helping people to remember the original worth of energy interaction. If you truly understand what an energy interaction really is, one of the laws of this reality, then you don't have to be afraid that you will want for anything.

At this moment a lot of people find themselves in a mental stalemate; to keep doing what they do otherwise they won't be able to keep up their standard of living or may even fall back in this. Fear drives them. Taking the step from fearful thoughts (ego) to faith, in other words surrendering to life (Self) asks you to detach from money as necessity for your right of existence. I don't mean that money is dirty and that you should turn your back on it. You don't need to let anything go, only your identification and grabbing it out of fear. You are being asked to look at your relationship with money, as at this moment it's a clear symbol of the ego. Look at how friendships, family relationships and relations change from love to hate when money is involved. What leads you? This is standing eye to eye facing the ego. Are you being led by fear or by insight?

A person who is truly him or herSelf and gives expression to the passion in him/herSelf has, energetically speaking, a powerful outgoing energy.

Powerful, outgoing energy can only attract the same. Because money is an energy form, your needs will always be met and it is highly unlikely that you'll totally be without if you are Yourself. It could be that you have nothing because your Self wants to become unattached, for instance when you transmit fear of losing it. This is an energy logic; if you transmit 'I don't have enough' then the universe will give you what you ask.
The change in our attitude to money as a natural manifestation of what we transmit still requires a transition period, one in which more and more social patterns will break down and more and more creative initiatives will arise. They will be aligned to the 'whole-being' of humans who are working together with the laws of this reality.
If you look at money as energy then it has no worth and it can be freed from your fear, freed from your pursuit of it. And then it can flow. Energy is movement, hoarding is stagnating the flow. It is a means not a goal. When you place money as a goal outside yourSelf then it will never flow, because the expansion power expands from the here and now. The abundance begins from inside! When abundance flows from yourself it's a logical attraction and a means to manifest abundance, one in which money is not always needed. Discovering abundance hasn't always to do with money makes space for another perspective on money.

Imagine that we've been freed of money, how would the world look? Every human on this earth is completely unique and will offer the world unique creations and services, each from a different alignment. You have people who find their passion in the contact with mother earth and they do their part in this. People who look after the technological development, people who look after children in order to bring insights. There is no one too many. We're all tools to keep and evolve the human race. Everything you need to express your unicity you attract energetically and you will, when money is no longer needed attract the services and creations of other people who give you what you need and the other way around.

This doesn't necessarily have to happen by swapping services. Because if we look from unity then it doesn't matter where the energy comes from, where it goes and if you personally benefit from it. It's bestowing your creations on the world, because you love giving expression to yourself. When the ego settles down and unity is clear then there isn't a 'me' and 'mine' and keeping a 'mine' safe which would stagnate the flow.

There will only be serviceability to the field of unity and then something can really start to change. The realization that Unity is what we are, is absolutely *necessary* if change wants to be realised.

It's not plausible that this will be realized just like that. It's more possible that there will be a shift, an intermediate form in which people will become more important than profits. Making use of the moment instead of setting goals. The heart above the ego. The Now (projects) above later (prognosis). This change is already taking place and it's beautiful to see and beautiful to work with. So don't feel dispirited that the place you earn your money doesn't match with how you experience life, be the change. Know that this is only possible through a pure connection with yourself and therefore with the universe. That's why the personality has to let go of the illusion of control, to start focussing on the real energy flow. Free from the grip of fear and loss. Out of our dependence on money as necessity for the security of our existence. You are your security. Everything originates from you and this reality with its laws is your playing field.

THE MANIFEST

THIS
WORLD
IS THE MOST
WONDERFUL
DIVINE
PROJECTION

The world around you is a 360 degree film screen with you as absolute midpoint.
Everything originates from you. Everything you see and experience you only see because it resonates with your consciousness. You see it because you look through specific glasses; the ego. Without these glasses this reality would not exist. So there is nothing wrong with the ego! It has a bridge function between the ever present Consciousness and this reality. Everything you see, hear and feel in interaction with other people and situations in the world appear *from* you and for you as reflection of you. You are the heart of the universe in which this unfolds and takes place. Even if the body you find yourself in moves a meter, a kilometre or moves in longitude you are and will always be the midpoint from which everything appears. In the figure at page 41 you can see that the manifest, the world of the form, is an extension of you; of the spiritual heart, which penetrates in deeper and denser physical layers of the manifest.

Nothing in this World is real, only Brahman is real.
The World is Brahman.

This well-known statement by Ramana Maharashi, a spiritual sage from India, gives an image of what the world is and how beautiful it is.
Nothing in this world is real, only God is real. Everything in this world is an illusion, a projected light bundle that is ever changing. The ego is the projector. God is the only all omnipresent; the observer and creator of the projections.
The world is God. It took a long time for me to understand this. Only when I really saw it for what it truly was did I make the click. The world is the most wondrous Divine projection. Everything that is subtly driven by the spiritual heart, as a thought comes up inside you and forms itself in your energy system, it will eventually become visible in the world of form. It's an illusion that 'you' as personality are the one determining, it's the Divine. It's originated from the field of Unity and travels through the vessel of you as a person.
Without the energetic support of Consciousness this image would dissolve back into awareness.
This means that what we see isn't personal. Through our spiritual Self we are connected as One and through this connection there is a

collective consciousness (read: collective belief system), why we see a tree for instance when we see a tree (although on the human level we all experience it in a different way through our human senses, which are the 'glasses' we look through). This sounds logical but the other way around is also possible, because that what hasn't yet filtered into our consciousness we can't see.
A lot of things in this world are exactly the other way around than we thought. I will only believe it if I see it, is what you sometimes hear, but actually it is exactly the other way around: You see it because you believe it (or because it is a collective belief). That's why we're limited in our creating to the scope of what we can imagine.

All the personal layers we experience (-the earthly bodies-) are connected to this earthly reality. Outside the earth-bound reality there is no personal experience anymore. That's why everything you see in this world and what is manifested in this world only becomes visible because it has gone through our ego funnel; our belief system. Insight into the nature of this reality, the manifest, is therefore vital for the evolution of human kind. This is how faith or belief systems get stretched out, and things can become possible that we never thought were possible with more limited glasses. We're ready for an evolutionary step. Living together in the NOW and from the NOW in creating a whole new society. (This subject will be covered more extensively in the book ' The global consequences of our dualistic ego').

Exercise:

Find a spot, either in your living room but even more interesting is somewhere in nature or where there are lots of people.

Shut your eyes and feel how you are the centre of where you are. You are the midpoint. Then open your eyes and make a frame with your hands. This frame helps you to see as if you were looking at a film. A film that is being projected from you as projector.

What do you see? It's not about your interpretation of what you see but you experiencing yourself as midpoint and of your ego as funnel.

Also turn around. Look at the whole moving screen. Maybe people come by, or animals, or you see shops, houses...

Everything you see is You and your perception of what you see. Can you feel how you are the midpoint, even if you move a meter to the left?

—

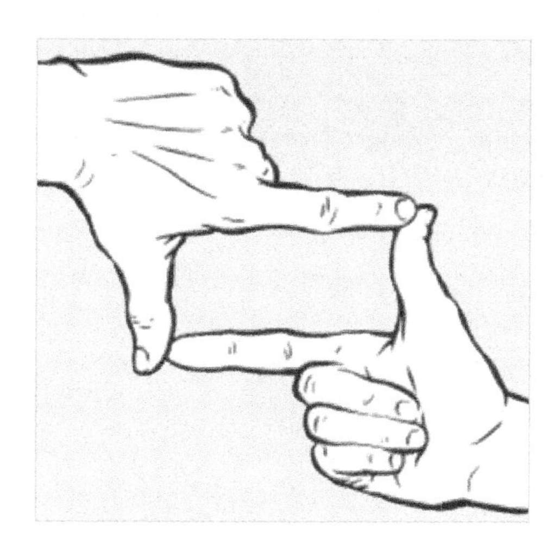

MOTHER EARTH AND YOUR EXISTENCE

DO YOU REALLY WANT TO BE HERE?

We're going to look at the earth at a deeper level; by feeling.
I often meet people who, as you call it, are not grounded. They are not here and are cut off from their Self. They have retracted themselves from existence or have never fully embraced their existence. If you have ever had the luck to meet a Self-realised person then you may have been aware that this person is fully present in the here and now. Fully grounded and okay with existence.

Coming home in yourSelf is coming home on earth

By merging with yourSelf your heart opens and simultaneously your crown and first chakra open. The quickest way to a good grounding is through an open heart. By which you choose (anew) for life. Living in this reality on the earth in this moment. This moment that wants to fully be embraced and experienced exactly as it is with all your senses. Look at your relationship to the earth. This simple fact can be a real test case for many people. From a religious standpoint but also by people who wander around in the 'new age' circuit (which can also be called a sort of religion) is the promise of a loving afterlife or a loving world on the other side. But Jesus didn't say that heaven is here on earth for nothing. Do you really want to be on this earth?

The resistance against the earth and your existence is a resistance to the here and Now, a resistance against your own and the collective projections in this world. It's not all that strange that nearly all of mankind has lost the connection with mother earth. This is a result of the disconnection to ourSelf. The ego has become the leader and is the reason why we suffer. The ego that can never be in the here and now because it is a thinking mechanism and thoughts are always about then and soon.
Re-establishing contact with mother earth and mother herself (!) has everything to do with transcending the ego which is based on an enormous misconception 'I am not good enough, this here and now is not okay'. It all boils down to Self-acceptation. Your doorway to Love is fully accepting yourself, the other *and* the manifest. Being fully present with, and allowing all your senses to experience all sensations in this present moment. Becoming spiritually mature has nothing to do with lingering in multi-dimensional regions but being present in this Now.

Multi-dimensional travel is only possible from a total merging with the here and now.
We have two hearts. The spiritual heart that is connected to father Consciousness (at the level of your heart chakra, next to your physical heart) and the earthly heart that is connected to the centre of mother earth. This earthly heart, as I experience it, is situated just under the belly button.

In many cases there is a correlation between your relationship to the earth and your relationship to your mother. Your biological mother is the one who gave you this earthly existence. The relationship to your mother represents your relationship to your existence in the world and also wants you to shine your light on it. The projections on it want to be neutralized. Are you okay with your existence on this earth? With the existence that you received from her? Were you able to receive her care? Do you long to go back to her? Is there resistance to her? Stories want to be neutralized and desires internalized. When there is acceptance of her (the other) then you will see that your disconnection with mother can transform into a conscious connection to the archetype mother and to Mother Nature.

Mother Nature is the nurturing, opening, feminine aspect in this world. To let yourself be carried by her asks surrender. Some people experience this in nature as it is her nature to embrace you without judgment. Nature stills thought, she doesn't expect anything, she doesn't control anything, she only sways with everything that comes and goes and stays nurturingly present. Do you know the feeling of being carried by a bed of grass, the experience of a rustling tree that gives shadow from the heat, of the flower who gives you her beauty, the berry bush that gives you food and the water from the sea that embraces you and carries you back to the land?
It's at these moments that the ego subsides and surrenders to the Heart. Mother earth is abundant.

All that is manifest in this world is made from natural resources from mother earth. In all material things there is a little bit of her, not only in the flora and fauna. All that has manifested is a collaboration between the male and female, mother earth and father consciousness, the heart and the spirit. Only when we reconnect to the feminine and we re-establish the balance, will this world be the kingdom which Jesus implied, because all manifestations first need to go through the funnel of your and our collective projector. So don't deny the ego or the world but accept and respect both for what they truly are; in service of you as creation of you!

LIFE DETERMINES

WHAT'S ADDRESSED
COMES FIRST
AND WHAT THAT IS
YOU WILL SEE UNFOLD

The life situations you encounter are a projection of the things that have the most priority in your life. This is dependent of which level your consciousness is at. Or, in other words; if you're still moving towards yourself or if you already are yourself and are in service of the field of Unity. It's very logical that what has the most priority becomes visible, because what you transmit in energy; your fears, your passion and your non-acceptance are being manifested and reflected in your life situations.
Let me make this more clear by showing you a few of the possible projections you may encounter can show you.

- **That what withholds you to be who you are.**
  The natural flow is always in the direction of yourself and the expression of this self. If you're still covered with ego-dust then this is what's reflected; what withholds you the most in being who you are. The biggest counteracting energy, the strongest non acceptation is logically that where most of the focus lies and thus what you transmit and receive. What you repress in yourself will be expressed in the outside world.
  What you will ultimately encounter are your deepest fears and your shadow because they are in the cooking pot and want to be let out. These are potentials that want to be used, not negative qualities - that's what you thought of them. When this shadow comes into your light they no longer stand in the shadow and then the quality can be lived to its fullest potential.

- **That what helps you to live your fullest potential.**
  Once you have accepted yourSelf and there is no longer any rejection of who you are, life will start resonating on your deepest desires, the wishes of the heart, on the energy timbre of your True Self. Life will make this visible, which will help you to align with your fullest potential. In this phase which form truly belongs to you wants to be crystalized. That's why for a while distorted manifestations still become visible even when you're already aligned with yourself. Because your life was built up from a character that you played for your safety and security and is now resonating on who your truly are, which is often a completely other person than before. This is also a story about energy: the

crystallization is letting the flow of your true Self completely free. But this flow will still come across remnants of beliefs which are still in the way to you living your fullest potential. Even if it's no longer necessary to keep this belief alive then it could be that this wants to become visible so that the mind expands and projections are able to form from who you really are.

- **Where you play your role in service of the field of Unity.**
  When you're fully transparent then personal interests will move more and more to the background and you will start living in synchronicity with what is in service to the collective field and where you have a role to play in it. I will cover this more fully later on.
  Where you resonate in energy will always become visible. So don't avoid anything and allow everything into your heart as the observer. Today, In this Now!

PROCESSES

THIS TOO SHALL PASS ...

Life situations and interactions with other people influence and act on the lack of freedom in you or in what wants to develop, in short, they start up a process and processes keep on coming and going as long as you wander around on earth. Everything in this world is being driven by the force of development. What I often see and therefore especially want to make clear is that people run off with these processes. You feel that something moves, something that is not familiar and maybe even unpleasant. That's when the mind wants to interpret what's happening assuming that with a diagnosis it can influence the process or quicken it. But in this way you interfere with the natural flow!

It's also getting used to just having stepped over the hurdle and to live from a whole new perspective, even if it's a lot more natural than from the ego perspective. For most people an inner process usually hits the button 'this has to go'. Change is not safe. But when you look from the observer there is no label of good or bad and also not about processes. You will notice that a process is just moving energy which you can't stop. It frees things up and loosens them. A process is good news! It drives you forward. So let it be. Take the rest that you need and look in awe at all the changing projections when a process has reached its purpose.

THE NOW, THE MAGICIAN'S TERRAIN

IN THE ABSOLUTE NOW
INTENTIONS ARE BORN
AS A SEED
FOR MANIFESTATION

You may be surprised that I haven't covered this topic earlier. That's because the Now sometimes gets misinterpreted. Its true meaning only becomes apparent once you have completely merged with the Now.

Since the term 'the Now' has gained popularity you see that people try and live a life in the Now. Where people first planned two years ahead, they make shorter plans, which is already a good way to let go of control, but is still control. The Now, as concept for happiness, is still a striving for something and doing your best to escape the Now.
Truly being in the Now is the dissolving of the illusion of 'me' and everything of ego; grabbing, protecting and wanting.
The *will* disintegrates in the Now. In the Now you transcend the ego-me, you are and always were freedom itself. There are no restrictions in time... in space. No control. Completely merging with the Now is merging with the nothing, with everything, with infinity.
It's the terrain of the Magician, the life conjurer, only from this perspective can you consciously participate in the play of life.
When you merge with the absolute Now you're in a null-point energy funnel from which all creation is deployed. But the irony is, there is no wanting to change anything anymore. You could only do this from service to the whole, not from personal gain.

In the now a natural overview takes place. From the absolute Now there is direct knowing because you are connected to the total field of Unity. You are everything and no longer chained to a personal will.
This human form has a special feature. The spiritual body is a link between this human reality and the infinite Consciousness. It is still in the early days, but from the absolute Now it's possible to travel using the spiritual body through all times, all distances and all dimensions. But only just as long as the person is alive. After the physical death there is no personal spiritual body any more. After physical death all the 'personal' merges with the greater awareness.

Stepping into the Now while you're in a human body is the key in being able to use a much greater potential than you ever thought possible. But watch out that the mind doesn't see this as a possibility to be superior! It is impossible from this position to enter the Now. This book only has the function to help you to step out of the concept Now, by stepping into the reality of the Now. And not feeding the ego with hope and desire. So be vigilant.

If we speak about the shift from a life holding onto safety and security, resulting from -then and -later, to a life swaying with the flow of life, from an anchoring in the Now, then themes which triggered you in the past dissolve, and I mean really dissolve! Even the events that happened before these things dissolve. In the Now, past and future dissolve. When themes let go of you, they literally disappear from the field, your memory disappears. The past has never taken place and this also applies for the collective pain and memories. Every moment we are repeating things, once we stop doing this, by merging with the Now, then it literally never took place.

THE CREATIVE FORCE

THE CREATIVE FORCE
FORMS A CONTINUUM WITH
TIME, FORM AND INTENTION

IT CREATES OUR REALITY

EVERY MOMENT

ANEW

There is only Now and in this Now everything happens simultaneously. Past, present and future, here and there. From this absolute Now a continual, creative force is at work which we call God, Consciousness, the Universe. But how does this work exactly?

Development is not linear but cyclical. There is a continual movement from the field of Unity. In every moment a new energy seed is born in the Now, fed by intention. It seeks a channel through which it can further penetrate in the material reality. Like throwing a pebble in a pond and watching the ripples grow ever wider. Not only in width but from all sides, centrifugal, in increasingly denser energy frequencies. It's like the prick of a pin, sending the complete energy field into movement.

This seed can only grow and flower in this reality because there's a human link between it. The ego!

The spiritual Self gives direction

Ego gives form

Consciousness carries

The seed appears even before it arises in your thoughts and the field is set in motion. All connected lives, levels and other essences will be influenced by this and will sway with it. Because everything will always unfold in this Now, nothing is determined. There are no limits, no provisions in time, only energetic intentions.
When the energy increasingly takes on a more material form then there is no limit to the possibilities; the well-known butterfly who moves its wings can bring about a hurricane. Everything the ego can think of is possible (but not controllable).
In this whole creation process the ego has an important function. Your essence cannot get around your ego! That's why it is necessary to broaden your mind so this process can run freely and what's manifested can be aligned to who you truly are.

Manifesting is energy that has become form

That's what life situations are for, to give you insights. Insights expand the mind. It's wondrous to look at the world from this knowing; to how and what is being manifested from you. Knowing that it's already present in your energy field before you became conscious of it!
We therefore essentially live in the past. If you want to stop what's happening you're already too late, because the seed is already growing. You are only asked to let it move freely. Open minded, what a great expression!

PART IV

YOUR RELATIONSHIP

AND SERVICE TO THE FIELD OF UNITY

UNITY

THE SENSE
OF ONENESS
IS THE FOUNDATION
OF A NEW WAY
OF LIVING (TOGETHER)

You've often heard me talking about the field of Unity. We saw in the last chapter how a pebble falling into water creates ripples in the energy field and penetrates increasingly deeper layers, and that this arises from a personal manifestation as midpoint. This reality is visible to us because there's a human ego that intervenes. But there are more people in this reality all connected via their spiritual body (or soul) with an infinite, expansive field. This is what I call the field of Unity. The place where the pebbles are thrown!

That's how something can be set in motion via one person and be picked up by the next who builds further on it. According to which energy is the most suitable and the most expanded mind to manifest through. The photo illustrates what I mean.
Here is the same rule that movement not only takes place in the width but from all sides. Therefore we *never* develop alone. We also don't awaken alone. We are ONE Consciousness. No one is further than another, we just have different roles to play. We are all in this together. Only when we decide as collective Consciousness to bring about change will global change be possible. What happens in the world is a mirror of our collective consciousness.

You're probably asking yourself what happens when we reach the top of the cone of Consciousness. When we dissolve into Unity. But there is no end, just like you can infinitely multiply, you also can divide without limit. We are penetrating deeper and deeper into subtleties, ever more sophisticated and transparent.
There is only an end to it in our perception. It is the end of your view and then we create a new view and another perspective. We hitchhike along with evolution. Time falls away and everything that we have ever experienced is uplifted or in other words is permeated from a new viewpoint.
It loses more density. All of us 'do' this, as Unity. We are all part of the Unity and this is not to be ignored, it IS! Everything you still keep on repressing or develop and transform you do as a part of the Unity; and will therefore expand in energy from you to all surrounding energies. You don't awaken only for yourself but for everyone as Unity.

It's possible that a few people all receive the same insight at the same moment with the same content, one seen through the eyes of science, the other through the eyes of energy and yet again another through the eyes of someone cutting a carrot. This is a result of the 'water ripple' that penetrates and brings something into vibration by different people. But you still have to do with evolution. You can only build and ripple outwards on the fundaments of this here and Now. It will therefore always be a gradual process. We can't jump from A to Z, we need to take all the steps in between. This is comforting. You only have to take one step at a time. You can open yourself to subtle information from the collective field. When there are insights through this collective layer, they are able to make their way to the brain faster and be manifested. These layers are not (yet) visible to everyone and when your sense of perception is still limited to denser energy it's not tangible or it will be written off as having other causes. That's why this path is a path of increasingly subtler observing, from feeling (feelingly observing).

What needs to be clear is there is no goal, in the way we would formulate it from the ego. We don't have to determine anything and don't have to go anywhere. Everything in this reality has arisen from Love, from a natural expansive force. A force of creation that sees no difference which way it develops, we are free in this. But there is a whole web of Essences working together to manifest a communal intention, with this reality as a sort of creative project. You could see this as a goal but not in the common sense of the word. There is no deadline, no punishment if it isn't reached. It is a game, love, passion.

The awareness of Unity and of our spiritual Self is needed in order to see that all development manifests in this manner. Faster than fast is not possible. Chasing goals that don't align with deeper intentions neither. You can't force it by wanting it.
Truly working together with Essence, with Unity and with Source means being receptive and placing your personality, body/mind system at its service. Not as something that wants to interfere with and take over control. It's just too big, too beautiful...
This field of unity of which we are all a piece of Consciousness has an enormous potential, a driving force of creation, every moment anew. From all midpoints...
Imagine the possibilities that are available if the realization of Unity would be collective! When we no longer look from 'me', but truly realize that we are in service to a 'we' as One. Self-Love for everything as One...

COMPASSION

SUFFERING IS SEPARATED
COMPASSION IS CONNECTED

We are One Consciousness. In merging with the Now we can align our spiritual body to every level of consciousness, every life and every experience.
It seems to many people that we have many past lives but in reality all those lives unfold at the same time and outside this human manifestation there is no individuality at all. What we call the soul is the spiritual body (which you can see in the diagram at page 41.) This also appears in an 'illusionary' layer of consciousness. You are neither your personal soul.

Don't be shocked, I'm opening a kettle of fish here. Most people believe in a separate soul that lives for ever. But also from the idea of multiple souls there is still an 'I-soul' (my-soul) and another soul and thus no Oneness. This level also wants to be seen as a reality that we experience but it isn't the absolute truth. Be assured it's even more interesting than you thought. We are all one soul. You are Consciousness itself, with experiences on different levels of consciousness.

When something resonates in the energy level on which your human manifestation vibrates through the spiritual body, via the field of unity, via the Now you can connect with everything and 'everyone' with the same vibration level.
What can become visible are images which come up, mind associations and projections from other levels of consciousness. It may seem that this could be from a past life. But in reality this all takes place in the Now in another manifestation of You as Consciousness. Not from you as individual soul but from You as Consciousness. You live everything simultaneously. You live all lives, all people. Now.

True compassion is connected through this Now to everything and everyone because you *are* everything and everyone.

Therefore not one experience is strange to you. You experience everything at once in this moment.

Feeling sorry for someone is another story. That's the ego that can imagine *that*... And *that* is something terrible, something which the ego thinks it will be very unhappy about if it were to happen. Feeling sorry for someone is making someone else's story our own by which we feed the my-mechanism

Just to go back to your connection to all people and all lives. Once you arrive on this terrain you can come across a lot of resistance, because from the personality, which only wants to be happy and have nice feelings, it doesn't want someone else's shit. And rightly so because it's not what is lived through you, so you don't have to carry it from a false sense of compassion.

What I often hear and see is that people want to shut themselves off of energy that they feel around or in other people. But that's not possible. We are all connected! What you're doing when you cut yourself off of 'someone else's' energy is that you repress this energy in yourself. Because what resonates in you and what you don't want to feel is a non-acceptation in yourself. Everything wants to be embraced. Also the person who suffers. As soon as something enters your script and it resonates in you, you are a piece of it and a link.

It makes sense that Buddhists speak of compassion as the starting point for another world. However do realise that compassion is not something you can do. It is the realisation that lights up when you merge with the Now.

EMOTIONAL INDIFFERENCE

WHERE EMOTIONS
HAVE BEEN SEEN THROUGH
THE HEART
CAN FLOW
FREELY

It may seem that when we're less emotion-led, we're indifferent to human suffering.
This is a recurring point of confusion we encounter as part of our process of awakening. Indifference is however, not really the case. In becoming more aligned with yourself you also become more open to what is really happening; you start seeing through the ego stories. You are no longer sensitive to the drama other people stage because you see their shining inner core; who they really are.
Often the energy in this moment feels fine but the story that is being told in this moment doesn't coincide with the energy. It could even be so, and maybe you've noticed this, that you have to laugh inwardly and at the same time as tell a sad story to a friend (as a voice in your head is holding you back in surrendering to laughing because you have to keep the story intact). Of course you don't want to contradict what you had so convincingly deposited earlier, you aren't someone who talks gibberish.

A transition is taking place from the ego to the heart, from emotion led life to sincerely resonating with what IS. You no longer explain suffering as 'imagine if that would happen to me' and thus, this component falls away. During your awakening you may come across a change in your emphatic feelings. It no longer does anything to you when someone tells you his or her drama. Be comforted that your humanity is only increasing. When someone is truly sad everything in you also cries because this is an expression of what IS and you are part of it in that moment.
From the viewpoint of Self you don't help another person by fuelling and confirming the drama stories. But if you are eye to eye with true suffering, in that moment you are the co-transformer of that suffering. But only if you don't make the feeling 'mine'.

So, try and see what is true and what is a drama story. This is a bit tricky because what gets confusing are all the beliefs about a better world and being a kinder more loving human being. The 'I should feel this is terrible' or 'I should be hugging the other person now' or 'it's not good that there's so much suffering'; these all want to be seen through. These thoughts create emotions because they don't coincide with your image of how the world has to be. But can you really know what the motivation of the Self is in attracting all these experiences?

A short time ago I met some people with a loved one who had been diagnosed with a terminal illness. These are moments of great shock. One person said that it surprised him that he wasn't worried. What was evident was that he had never really felt much of a connection with the person until now. It relayed how his perspective had changed from the horizontal line in worrying about later (based on then), to the vertical line of living in this moment.
In these moments when everything you thought safe, falls away the heart wholly opens. These are periods in which a deep connection between loved ones arise, a connection that never felt so deep. Situations in which your humanity is kissed awake; unless you don't fall into the seduction of the ego and shut yourself off or you feel a victim or you carry on with the 'I am my drama'.

Only from true compassion, from looking through the eyes of the heart, from the space where everything has already been accepted and nothing needs to be done, can true change take place on a small or on a great scale. Because change is constant. So, be true to the resonance of your heart and not to the drama, in doing this you become the pebble which ripples the water and touches the surroundings. You don't have to contradict or fight it, just let it subside in the space of your heart and give it room to do what wants to be lived through you.

NOTHING IS PERSONAL

NOTHING
IS REALLY PERSONAL

EVERYTHING
ORIGINATES
FROM THE SELF

The Self that wants to experience itSelf through human thoughts, human feelings and the human body in a world of polarities. The suffering we looked at in the last chapter is neither yours, nor someone else's. It comes through you and through the other as you are both a channel through which it can express itself. It only becomes suffering if you make it yours.
Once you realise we as One live every human experience and this reality is a playground in which this can take place, all your experiences will look different. You no longer have to compare what you are experiencing to what someone else experiences. Both of you do this by *living through* your personal manifestation experiences for the *field* of Unity. There can be real thankfulness for what someone else is experiencing. True understanding and compassion can arise when you no longer see the experiences as yours or someone else's, but *yours* as One. Can you feel how you then zoom out to another perspective? Out of the personal mode?

We're now coming to a phase in which personal pain-points dissolve and you no longer function at this level. You are a transparent channel through which collective pain is regulated. The earth only needs a few people to heal, when we stop making feelings and situations personal.

Experiences are not *yours*, they come *through* you!

You are a part of this Unity and your personal desires are subordinate. This may sound a bit impetuous but by reading the next chapters you'll see how well 'looked after' everything is. When you are fully yourself then precisely that which wants to be lived will come through you, not only for you but for all concerned! We are all connected and Consciousness will always manifest situations that are most serving to all concerned.

For you as Consciousness it doesn't matter who lives what. If I explain this at a group level, (when people come together) then what will be experienced is needed for all concerned, through the person who is the most suited for this energy and openness. The more transparent the attendees are the less distorted it will be manifested.

An example: You're at a meeting in which the deeper intention of the people attending is to awaken and to make visible what holds them back the most. In most cases the people attending are not aware of these intentions on a personal level.
Imagine in this case that it's about a family gathering. Sometimes igniting a bomb is needed to awaken and it can therefore be possible that someone (maybe even you) suddenly feels the urge to bring up a long hidden secret. Someone else will possibly live the sadness that accompanied this cramping by crying and therefore cleansing it. What may look like a family drama could in reality be a process of bringing into the light and healing what is blocking the people concerned in freely being themSelves, whereby the field of Unity becomes lighter. On a personal level you could point to a perpetrator (the person who brought the message) or a victim (the person who cried) but this is not what IS. It's not personal. This is what wanted to become visible and you were both the most suited to play a role in this. It got played out *through* you.

FOLLOWING WHAT *IS*

FOLLOWING
WHAT
IS

IS HONOURING
THE TRUE
REALITY

This means that we're moving towards and are beginning to observe from another level and that we're going to resonate on a more subtle level. Spiritual awakening is associated with increasing your energy frequency, breaking free from denser levels of material thought and entering into the subtler levels of feeling. Making it possible to recognise and follow the energy flow of this moment, seeing its true beauty, perfection and potential.

Let me give you an example. You're at your work and suddenly feel an enormous, inspired drive to write about something. You see it clearly and the flow wants to be carried out. Just at that moment your boss steps into the room and tells you there's a free place in a workshop you wanted to attend and he's letting you go... right now. Help! Oh dear... a hitch, because the energy coming to you is completely different to the movement of energy wanting to be carried out. Normally you wouldn't say no to such a chance, especially not from your boss. And don't look a gift horse in the mouth... but if the wave is coming then you have to surf! Go with the wave. If you let it pass by then you have to wait until the next wave. It makes no sense to push what you wanted to write out without drive or inspiration. When you try and use energy that wants to be carried out and also try and receive information then there's a big chance it won't land. Once you no longer interfere with the flow there will only be one option and that is to keep on writing. And trust that what you thought you had to learn at the workshop will come to you in another way, *if* it's important to you.

Another example; you've gone to bed early because your body needs sleep. Your body relaxes and the energy which is present in this moment spreads out and settles down to rest. Then your partner comes into the room and wants to seduce you into making love, something you really wanted the last couple of days. But if you were truly honest with yourself then this moment is not one for prickled action, but for sleep...

Following what IS, is being completely true to yourSelf.

And transcending the ego. The beautiful thing about following this flow is that you will always be cared for. Not by a God or Angels outside you. It's logical; you follow the energy of this moment and therefore you give space to what has the most priority for you *and* for the field of Unity. You have no idea why this is important, but it's not about you as a person. You will eventually realise that your service to the field of Unity gives far more satisfaction than chasing after personal gain.

For instance in the last example; who knows if through this story insights and manifestations will arise that will lead you to what you wanted to do here. Let's call this your calling. Perhaps, like the second example, sleep may be the missing link through which your body is permanently and naturally orgasmic and you therefore transcend the vice of desiring after sexuality and create an opening to the field of Unity.

The starting point of true service to the Self is:

1. **Transcending the ego**
   (no longer living from apparent personal needs)

2. **Following the flow that comes from you and wants to be lived through you**

This is effortless and fun! You no longer have to do your best to get something or to become something. You only have to open yourself to what IS and what wants to unfold in this moment through you. It's surrendering to the Now. In service of the Self. Life from this mode is a lot more playful than what the serious ego has made it. It encompasses an enormous potential of expression to *life* itself. The Self wants to shine its Light every moment anew in this reality, via you.

YOUR CALLING

NOT FORM
BUT BEING

People often ask me: What is my calling? As if finding a calling will bring you the happiness you always sought, the ultimate goal. It has however a grain of truth because if you do what you came here to do then that brings happiness. But if you turn it around and make your calling a goal for happiness then you miss an important step, namely:

YOUR CALLING IS WHO YOU ARE

You are your calling! Your calling is not a form, not work but it's who you are.
Simply by existing, you send out a certain energy that touches something in others. Whatever you do, in whatever form you pour it and wherever you are, what's so unique about you will always shine and resonate in the world and in the person who needs it right now. So you need not do anything and even then you're special and you have a role to play. Step 1 is to *be* yourSelf. After this we pour this Self into a form. When you let everything free, and have no more reserves, just by being yourself in everything you do and say or don't do and don't say, purely being your present energy, precisely being why you are here. Through your energy your Essence penetrates everything around you. If you're here to bring laughter, then you will instigate this in the energy field of the other via your energy vibration. If you're here to uncover where people are still unfree then that will happen. Maybe you hadn't recognised it as such, because it constantly had another consequence, but if this is your role, then this is your role. What matches your energy will flow through you and at the same time you're aiding the field of Unity. It's that simple!

I've met a lot of people and every time I'm in awe of the Essence of all these pieces of Consciousness. When the ego dust fell away and the True Self became visible I got a glimpse of this pure form and what I saw was different every time. For instance someone with the energy to connect differences. Someone who put their caring arms around people. Someone who gets things going. The steadfast pillar of strength. Someone whose role it is to live Love in a unique way. Someone who brought laughter, the grounding. Who keeps a fresh view on things. All unique energies only by *being*; spreading their gifts.

It is almost impossible to put into words how this service gives you fulfilment. For me it felt a lot similar to when I fantasized about finding my other half. The bliss in coming home and giving expression to your Love.

When you arrived in this reality you came with certain intentions. Via this manifestation in the form of you, you wanted to experience certain themes and from your unique alignment be of service to the field of Unity. You stepped into a personality with certain traits, some of which you had thought to be useless, or even difficult, but seemed to be exactly the traits you needed to fulfil your role.

You will always remain human. Even awakening spiritually will not relieve you of your humanity and this is not even desirable. Take for instance perfectionism. The energetic worth of this trait could be having an eye for quality. It's annoying to you that you exaggerate it and you identify with the outcome. But pursuing quality, because you love quality, is a trait that can be very meaningful in what you have to do here. That's why accepting yourself totally is so important, so your qualities can just do their 'work'.

Or take for instance a spicy temperament. This can be quite trying for people because they often experience resistance to their expressions. But if this is allowed to be, then exactly through these sorts of qualities Consciousness is able to throw bombs and awaken other people out of their dream. Or it can give you the role of inspirator, the one who lights the candle in the hearts of others. This drive is exactly what's needed in a situation or in a group. The role of getting things done because a lot of people tend to 'stay put'.
Whatever you came to do and to give, it will always fit with the human vessel in which you house. So just be yourself!

The form in which you can best express yourSelf will find its 'form' when you start following your passion.

SELF-EXPRESSION

FROM BEING
TO FORM

Just *being* and above all; letting yourSelf be, is resting in Love. By nature we're living in a reality of polarities in which the Self is expressed in a form. What it's all about in this reality is Self-expression. The expression of the Self. This will bring you the most joy.

I would therefore like to point out the difference between how the ego expresses itself and how Self expresses itself.

- **Repressing versus expressing (acting out)**
  What we discovered at the beginning of this course is that the ego wants to escape the Now. It doesn't want to feel the sensations of life and therefore represses or expresses them. This form of expressing such as acting out emotions is not the Self-expression I mean. This will not bring you the joy that Self-expression gives. It will probably only help by releasing your stress.

- **Expression of the Self**
  Self-expression is a form of expression that transcends cramped reactions. It's a free flow from the Heart that wants to be manifested; in image, in sound, in service and in forms which touch the heart.

The wondrous thing about self-expression is when something is sincerely and fully expressed and if it's totally aligned with the energy of the moment then the heart will open. Your heart as well as the other person(s) who observe this form of expression. This is truly magical. You might have experienced this when listening to a piece of music and felt that your heart opened. Or if you see a painting that touches you or hear a speech by someone who really speaks from the Heart.

When you live from the heart then an enormous outflowing energy is emitted that attracts the same energetic power. Therefore the expression of yourself is precisely what your unique role is in the world and in which you can provide for yourself in life. Your calling is You poured into a form.

People sometimes say, 'if you have a gift then you shouldn't ask money for it'. In truth, where your heart is and what comes from your heart is what you're really good at and it wants to flow, outwards and inwards. Whether you're a plumber, nurse or inspirator. Everyone's role is precious. To the ego it will seem strange that you're making your work from who you are, because it unfolds so effortlessly. The ego still thinks it needs to work really hard to be worth something.

Expressing yourSelf and doing what you came here to do gives an enormous fulfilment because you're living your fullest potential. You are in service of what your Self wanted to live and nothing can hamper that. It nourishes and gives joy because you're wholly yourSelf and you express yourself in exactly what you most love to do.

Exercise:

You can do this exercise on your own but it's better to do it with someone else.

In this reality sound is a beautiful medium to express ourselves with. I offer this because everyone knows that sound has an energy vibration. This exercise will teach you, by following the energy flow to connect with yourSelf. When you fully express yourself in sound; with pitch, tone and voice then you are aligned to what you experience in this moment and your heart will open.

Sit opposite each other and look at each other's left eye (or choose a place where you can be alone without being disturbed).
Maybe you're already completely open and can immediately look into the eyes of Source, maybe you need to let go of the ego chatter in order to relax in the Now. Take the time to embrace all your projections without judgment.

One of you will now express all the sensations that arise by sounding. Look for the right tone, timbre and the right volume until you've found all the right frequencies and it matches what you feel in this moment. You will discover that the heart opens... and that your sensations and experiences are free.

The other person stays observing. For the observer it's important not to give advice, only receive and feel what the other gives you. When the right resonance is found you will also be touched in your Heart.

Be aware that you don't start singing a known melody. This shuts off your openness to the changes in energy that come up in every moment.

—

Sound can evolve into words... Words into deeds...
You'll notice when you live sincerely from this surrender in daily life and what wants to be lived starts resonating, that not only others receive everything without judgement but that it has a force of attraction and it gives you a real sense of gratification.

YOUR GREATEST FEAR

WHERE YOUR
GREATEST FEAR LIES
YOU WILL FIND YOUR STRENGTH

Once we come to the point of living our fullest potential many people encounter their greatest fear. Stepping into your Light is, for one reason or another the most fearful experience there is. You will not only encounter a dying ego that felt secure by upholding illusions but you'll also probably encounter qualities that were repressed for many years. What was unique in you was repressed, because you excelled in it. You were not 'normal' in this, you were different. It was misunderstood by the ones who raised you and therefore you became afraid of that part of yourself. But, where your greatest fear lies... you will find your strength; this is where your greatest ecstasy lies.

Let's take a look inside and feel what's bursting to come out and be free. What wants to burst out but you're still trying to repress. The thing you keep hidden from the outside world, because you're afraid of how it will come out. That's where your potential lies!
Most probably life will start to mirror this, so you don't need to go and look for it. If something gets ignited then this is the moment to feelingly observe it. It only wants to be allowed to be, in this moment. Otherwise it will keep coming out in a distorted way and it just wants to flow freely. How...? You don't know this yet. Leave it over to life.

A lot of people are looking for quiet and inner peace because we run away from the disquiet in ourselves: a disquiet present within ourselves because what we are is not allowed to be. There is a big fear of the supposed darkness in our self. For that what we for whatever reason don't see as from ourselves, just while we were looking to becoming whole with our Self. What a paradox! The thing you run away from is exactly what you desired.
Whichever way you look at it, Truly being yourSelf is only possible when you behold this fear!

Know that what you're afraid of isn't a quality, but a thought *about* how this quality will express itself. The energetic worth of the trait is just something that belongs to you. The fear is the idea about how destructively it will express itself or how it will set you up for failure if you were to let it free. But when this energy no longer has a negative connotation for you then it can become the driving force behind the form you're going to pour yourSelf into.

SURRENDER

AND WHEN THERE IS NOTHING LEFT
TO REPRESS, TO GRAB OR
TO REPEAT INTO STORIES
THEN SURRENDER
IS THE LAST STEP TO TAKE

THE SURRENDER
OF THE PERSONALITY
TO YOURSELF

When you discover that everything you upheld was only based on false ideas and never really existed, then you can release the control you thought was necessary *over* these ideas and the form in which they became visible. The Self determines and life is a satisfying adventure: if you let yourself drift with the flow.

In fact, everything you think and everything you see in the outside world builds itself up every moment anew, and the whole projection breaks up every moment anew. Time and time again you build this illusion based on your ideas about the world. A divine process controlled by our Self. And from this expansive and creative mid-point we keep on developing as One Consciousness in this reality. Every unceasing moment.

Living in surrender to yourSelf is being in service of what wants to manifest and be lived through you and the field of Unity. Through this personality you can observe the miracle that takes place through you. We are making a unique journey through this reality.
Stop wanting to change it. You were born to shine. You don't have to do anything.

There are three stages in which Self-realisation unfolds (but not necessarily in this order):

- **Mind realisation:** on an intellectual level you have understood how it works, who you are and are not. There is pure insight, but it is possible that when realisation has only taken place at this level that life is still denied and controlled and the heart remains shut.

- **Heart realisation:** the heart opens for the outside world and feelings are allowed, but at this stage automatic patterns can still rise up through the interference of the ego. In this realisation you can still be stuck in the illusion of the 'me' and the 'other'. For instance: The other who is lovingly allowed.

- **Realisation of Being:** here you're completely aware on the level of the mind, the heart and in everything you are that the other truly does not exist. You are everything and as personality not controlling. You are the transparent tool through which heart energy flows into the world and you come to total Self-expression without the interference of the ego that wants to determine. In total cooperation with all the connected energies.

Or in other words, there are three paths to Enlightenment:

- **The path of the intellect**
- **The path of feelings**
- **Surrender**

Whichever path you choose (and they often cross each other) you will eventually totally surrender. The free fall into the mystery.

How does surrender feel?

I'll try and say something about this as many people have no idea what's waiting for them.
Through this, the beauty of this moment, that seems so strange, gets passed by and overruled by the ego. When you recognise the freedom of surrender it will be easier for you to stay awake in surrender and to point the ego to its rightful place. It's called freedom, but for a lot of people it feels bare, vulnerable, void, overwhelming and silent. The world loses its form. There is no longer a divide between you and another and the material world. It feels as if you are no longer here. As if you have dissolved. The framework of the 'me' was safe, known but also constrictive. Now there is space, almost too much space when you feel it for the first time. The things you thought were important before are no longer important. The convulsions of the ego trying to do its best to achieve seems like a small monster that's trying to keep you small. It is all good now. Nothing is needed anymore. It is quiet, peaceful, loving. Or actually more... blank. No good, no bad, blank. Inner peace. And with every breath you feel all of life flowing in and flowing out. Everything penetrates in every cell. Intense. Vibrant. Alive.

Often people are shocked by this completely different modus. I hope, when you recognise some of this, that you can stay conscious in it so the energy that is available in the moment can transform what is needed. Surrender is, being breathed into life. For you to receive.

PART V

TRAPS

THE SPIRITUAL EGO

**"I'VE PASSED THAT,
I HAVE NO EGO ANYMORE."**

~ PASSER BY ~

The whole process of awakening: awakening to what IS and to who you really are is a revolutionary step in a human life. It's an adventure with many blessings but also with difficult moments of detachment. And above all a lot of traps set by the ego to deceive you in order to secure its identity. That's why in the next chapters we're going to look at traps that occur during this process.

Trap nr. 1: *The spiritual ego*
Once you've tasted the bliss of surrender and have discovered that you are ubiquitous Consciousness then the only thing you want to do is to shout it out and share it with others. Great, because what the heart thinks... But ego often tones down the heart's wish to one of 'I am further than you and I'm going to tell you how it works'. It's very tempting to make your realisation an ego-thing and to push your insights onto others. You place yourself above other people and then you're trapped once again in a dualistic perspective of superiority and inferiority. Truly awakening is holding nothing and nobody as more or less than yourself!

No matter how upright your motivation may seem to persuade others to walk this path...(if everyone awakens then we'll have a brighter world), when you still want to change something in the outside world then you haven't yet integrated your realisation in truly seeing and being, that all of this is YOU and it is already accepted.
A spiritual ego can also summon a realisation from the past and elevate it into a success story through which, in this Now it perpetuates itself, a trophy it exhibits to enhance the glory of itself. The realisation has obviously become a memory and thus is not an actual realisation that continues in this Now. Awakening is not any experience at a certain moment in time, it is a permanent change in perspective.

Spiritual egos are difficult to penetrate because they have a shield around them and insights from other people are not permitted because they think they have already made it. If you sense this within you, feel how you harden and grant that the ego surrenders to the heart. Be completely honest to yourself. You are the only one who can be vigilant about this.
Luckily life will always make visible where you are not yet free, so please stay open to Self-inquiry. You don't have to surrender to someone else only to yourself.

MEANINGLESSNESS

"THE MEANING
OF LIFE
IS THAT
YOU'RE GOING FOR IT"

~ ALEXANDER SMIT ~

Trap nr. 2: ***the meaninglessness of life***
There is no advantage for the ego in awakening. It gets nothing in hand with which to feed itself. It loses its seat on the throne and literally doesn't know what's going on (as this isn't understandable on the level of the mind). Mind has no idea what it gets into once it walks this path.

When you step over the threshold from ego to being, you enter an area where there is no reason or meaning to life except life itself. Everything around you is illusion, but we don't yet see the beauty of the illusion. This can be very challenging for the ego. Why should I keep on doing what I'm doing? Is there absolutely nothing in which I can be useful? Something I can contribute to? Some people can really be imprisoned in this and even fall into a depression. So look out for this!
Depression which originates from seeking a meaning is being stuck in the idea that your existence has utility and is meaningful in a way that the ego can match with good or bad. It is a very fundamental feeling, especially when you ask people what the very worst is for them. And even more frightening is the thought 'then I am no one anymore'. 'Then my life had no purpose'. Meaninglessness can touch at a very deep level.

Then in a natural way the moment arrives that suddenly you have a great insight that there is no meaning in the true word of meaning. It can't be grabbed and poured into a form. The depression that comes from this moment of awakening doesn't come by the awakening itself, but because of confusion. The mind can't place it.
The ego is confused because it was looking for meaning for all those years. The ego had never imagined to come across this realisation.
The meaning of life is free of meaning. You can't comprehend this or understand it. Don't try to but let the mind dissolve in not-knowing. In this phase rest in no man's land, as long as needed without trying to grab for insights.

Discovering that you are nobody and that this world is an illusion and without meaning feels like the carpet being tugged out from under your feet. It's only the image of who you thought you were and thought the world was that has been dismantled, not who you truly are. This first shock is needed to awaken you.

Trying to give meaning to life was, from the very beginning a surrogate

in filling the emptiness of the disconnection to yourSelf. This dream has no meaning and that's why it's such a beautiful playground. You don't have to achieve anything, you may simply be.
When you truly look through the eyes of Self then there will no longer be any motivation to give meaning to life, because you have found something better!
Namely life itself! You are the meaning of life. This moment is the meaning of life. It encompasses everything.
Meaninglessness doesn't mean that you just give up and stay lying on the couch, or that you throw all luxury away and start to live a sober life. Free of meaning means you are free to be what life asks of you. To enjoy this and to be in awe of it. Not a 'me' who wants to live on, but recognizing the 'me' as a vessel to experience life. Not later but Now.

The meaning of life is not the means to an end. The meaning is the journey of life that unfolds from you. There is no path to Freedom, Freedom is the path. To see this is truly enjoying every moment that life unfolds whatever way it goes. Seeing it from the beauty of being underway... going nowhere.

YOUR LAST CERTAINTY

ALMOST FREE AS A BIRD...

Trap nr. 3: *wanting to hold onto your last certainty*
Just before they merge with themSelves I often see people running circles around themselves. There's something they would rather protect than let free. Your last certainty, your last fear, the last clutches to an identity. 'If I lose this then I will really be nobody, then I'll be outlawed by life and engulfed by it'. It's an enormous step to let go of your last certainty. But the only way to surrender and to truly be yourself is to completely step out of your protection mode.
Daring to be completely naked and 'vulnerable'. Showing yourSelf to others exactly as you are, *including* what you would rather hide. From a deep insight that everything is transitory, except You.

Do you still have something on your heart? Make sure you release it. Some people carry secrets with them for years and years, the reason why they always have to be on the alert that it won't be revealed. How long do you want to keep protecting, believing that you were wrong, and holding onto certainties that only imprison you?
There is nothing wrong with you! There is nothing wrong about this moment!

If you have nothing left to lose, then you're free. If there is nothing left to protect, you are open. With an open heart. Accessible to connecting, because you are in connection with yourself, with Love. Don't hold onto anything! Let it free. Let it go as it wants to go. Let it flow where it wants to flow.
It's detaching from your last certainty. And if it is a secret or something you're shameful about or still holding tight because of your income or your partner... set it free.

Maybe you can feel the ego writhing 'no, no no', because the Light of your true Self has almost enclosed it. Maybe there is still a reserve to being yourself; the unknown. And you choose your known certainty. People keep on turning circles around themselves, circles that keep getting smaller until it comes to rest in the middle. In the Now.
Why I'm talking about this is because insight is an important link in creating an opening in the matrix. Truly recognizing that you are walking circles around it can be a turning point in a certain protection mechanism.

CONSCIOUSNESS AS SOMETHING OUTSIDE YOU

IT ISN'T:
ME AND CONSCIOUSNESS

IT IS:
I AM CONSCIOUSNESS

Trap nr. 4: *Seeing Consciousness as something outside yourself*

One of the last beliefs that you can come across before merging with yourSelf is the idea that Consciousness is something outside yourself. A God or Spirit or something more Divine than yourself, that is loving, that looks after you and always wants the best for you. There is no separate 'me' from Consciousness. That's an illusion. It isn't: me *and* Consciousness, it's: I *am* Consciousness.

As long as you see Consciousness as something outside yourself you're still sailing the mode of hope and desire. Then there's a 'me' and Consciousness, duality. Therefore there's always something outside you which you place blame on or responsibility or something that can save you from sin and unhappiness. And as long as this carries on you're not living your fullest Self. Then you're not the midpoint. Ego has found a back door.

'God is good' is also an illusion that wants to be dismantled so that you can truly live life as it is. Consciousness is blank, it isn't good or bad. And the experiences in life aren't good or bad... they *are*. God is reality, that what IS, and no God will save you from it.

Within religions you often see that people pray to a God, this also happens in the world of spirituality. We desire the moment of surrender. We desire the great pardon of Spirit. It's a movement of grabbing from outside to inside. But to be truly free, redeemed of the ego, is knowing that you are Consciousness, the centre from which everything arises. There is no duality. Duality is an illusion. There is no 'from the outside in'. You are the midpoint from which everything arises. Not the other way around. If it seems the other way around then there is not yet insight into the fabrication of this reality. Yes you can experience duality on a certain level. But when you're truly awake you can never again deny that it's an illusion, in which the two-ness isn't separated.
Nothing and nobody is separate from you. There are no two (or more) only One.

Eureka, you don't have to explain yourSelf to anybody or anything, not to people or a God, everything that appears has arisen from you and will return back to you.

STUCK IN THE POSITION OF OBSERVER

LIFE IS ...
PARTICIPATING IN LIFE

Trap nr. 5: ***Stuck in the position of observer***
The last trap that I want to talk about is one I often see in phases during the awakening process, especially with people who don't yet understand all levels of non-duality or unity. These phases have no fixed order and not everybody comes across the same traps, or pitfalls.

Once you have discovered that you aren't this body, these thoughts or emotions but the observer of all this then there's a movement in which you 'zoom-out' and observe life. You look at it from a 'distance'. For some egos this is a simple getaway door to disengage with life as it wasn't their favourite place to be. To observe life from this perspective is safe. Energetically speaking, these people dissolve into nothingness. They realised: 'I am no one' and therefore they dissolve. You don't partake in life anymore and are no closer to life even with an open heart if you stay in this position. There is another step to take, namely this one:

You are the observer *in* the story

You are the higher consciousness, the observer and the person who experiences this reality. And that means being completely present. Of course it's important to first know the position of observer before you can experience from this, as you can't skip over the process of distancing yourself from your stories. But watch out you don't get stuck in this. Then you'll miss the greatest experience! The freedom to truly *live* from an open heart. Because life is participating in life, from the inside out! Fully!

To step back into life is a step in which you become centred. You become the central point, the mid-point. The energy withdraws from all dissociations into a powerful central funnel of light that shines from you into the world. That's where the joy of life begins, feeling good within your existence. The joy of *being*, of the *'I am'*

I = Consciousness
AM = Manifestation

Let me take you through this step by using an exercise:

Exercise:

Make a frame with your hands like you did before at page 169. To challenge yourSelf you could go somewhere where it's quite busy. Your work, on the street or when visiting someone. First hold the frame close to your face and pull yourSelf away from this life stage by pulling the frame away. Then you feel the position of the observer clearly arising.
Once you have become used to observing from a 'distance' then you pull the frame a bit closer. Stay feeling in the present.

At about fifteen centimetres there is a transition that can feel exciting. This is the transition where the frame disappears and you step into the mid-point of your existence.
For people who have an escape route via 'standing outside life' this may bring up unrest or even fear. Give this space and let it transform in your light.

Pull the frame even closer if it feels ok.
Feel how you centre and thus at the same time can fully participate in life as observer.
—

RESPONSIBILITY

AS LONG
AS WE PLACE RESPONSIBILITY
OUTSIDE OF OURSELVES
WE CAN
NEVER
FULLY COME
TO THE REALIZATION
OF UNITY

The thorniest issue people encounter when Unity becomes a reality is accepting their responsibility. I wouldn't call it a pitfall but an irrevocable challenge that goes hand in hand with becoming spiritually mature. A lot of people just don't want to take this.

The word has a rather nasty tone because it's associated with 'having to' and of carrying a load or whatever you feel concerning it. We don't actually want to grow up and take responsibility for what is manifested through us, but the fact is that is happening! You're hiding yourself and in denial when you keep on placing the responsibility on someone else, on the government or on a God outside you.
Of course you're not the only one from which is manifested, but as soon as something is disclosed through You it's your responsibility. You don't need to 'do' anything more than that.

I spent a long time over this point. Until the moment I realized that taking responsibility means that you truly connect with the role you have to fulfil. Saying 'Yes' to the fact that you as personality are a tool in service to what your Self wants to live, give and experience. This felt a bit weird because you as personality are not in control. By taking your responsibility, you sign your service to yourself. You stand completely behind everything that arises from you. If your role is to comfort or to shock, or if you give people an experience in forgiveness by causing something 'nasty' to happen, or by lending someone a hand out of the victim role... You take total responsibility for completely and congruently acting with the flow.

Everything that wants to manifest through you is your responsibility

This requires surrender at a very deep level. Not everybody comes to this point. It seems like a big step because it seems like you have a lot to 'lose': your innocence, maybe even your freedom. But this is only what the ego thinks of it. In reality this gives you freedom. True *freedom*. There is nothing and nobody outside yourself to which you need to justify yourself. Wherever you're standing in whichever way gets handled through you, you look from yourself at yourself and you play, live, laugh with yourself. You are angry, scared or sad about yourself and you help yourself if that is needed from compassion because that is what you love doing most.

But it asks of you to live very 'purely'. The more Consciousness the more responsibility. This also works on an energetic level. When you are disloyal to the flow then you'll get it even more violently and directly back. It requires more of you than simply acknowledging that you're responsible for everything that arises in your life.

Living on the margin of being and not being,
requires your vigilance every moment of the day.

Vigilance for the desires of the ego, for the greed and the drive to present yourself as more, better and more exclusive than the other. This is how you lose the connection with yourself.
With the Consciousness that has penetrated your existence there is just no other way. This path needs your vigilance until the last breath that the human body takes.

Your only direction is the flow from inside out. Not what your thoughts think of it. Even though it may seem strange, if you truly feel something from within, stay completely behind how you act.

VISION OF THE FUTURE

WHEN
AWAKENED CONSCIOUSNESS SHINES
THROUGH ALL PEOPLE
A WHOLE NEW CIVILIZATION
WILL ARISE

This is the evolutionary shift we as collective are now in. The transition to a new civilisation. Consciousness awakens and we are One Consciousness.
To describe a future you only need to describe how life is perceived from an awakened state of being and how human interactions take place without the interference of the ego. When that is the Now, that will be our future. It isn't a fairy tale, it's a logical continuation of the dream we're living, seen from another perspective and therefore also manifesting projections. But, this is only possible when we make the shift together and decide to make other choices...

- **Interpersonal relationships**
  The most important realisation is that we are not a 'me' and 'another' but One soul. This will stop the comparisons and also the judgments about different races. We're all in a human manifestation, in service of the field of unity. With this realization personal gain will fall away and a 'holy' respect will arise for everyone's separate choices. No control over each other anymore. No manipulations and abuse of power but room for all the roles that are played from the realisation: everyone has his/her own unique and special function inside the whole. The human being will be looked upon as a means to experience, play, to practice and to be cherished by this insight. We will see each other as brothers and sisters, everyone is equal, and everyone is special.

- **Language**
  Language will for the most part fall away because our experiences are direct and don't need to be talked about afterwards. Nor is it necessary to use language to try and tell someone how we think something should happen. There will be a lot more telepathic contact because we're all conscious of the prevailing energies. The realization that 'everything is energy' will be common knowledge and will make all superficial masks redundant because we look beyond this and feel. Language and material form will become more of an art form because the importance of it will fall away.

- **Mother earth**
  We will once again work together with the earth because we no longer ride against the tide of the prevailing energies. We will, because our energy is our guide, see how mother earth

energetically nourishes us and we wouldn't even think about destroying our own source of nourishment. The male and female will become aligned again.

- **Abundance**
  Greed will disappear as we will all come to recognise that greed only brings misery. There is insight that there is always abundance. Everything that's needed is here and we may receive it. Because there is abundance there will be no more grabbing for other people or things. People have come to Peace. The flow will reverse because we live from completeness, the grabbing from outside to the inside will change in giving from the inside to the outside.

- **Peacefulness**
  Living together with each other will therefore be automatically peaceful. There may be confrontations but.... only from a loving undertone, in service to each other with complete accordance to each other. Perhaps we'll find expression forms for the powerful side of ourselves but never destructive.

- **Institutions and rules**
  Rules and most institutes are no longer required. Government, church, police and prisons. We follow the rules of the heart and they 'punish' themselves where needed, but will always seamlessly fall together, because energy always seeks balance and always comes back to the zero-point. When people see that form is controlled and led by energy, then the energetic (natural) laws will be in place. Laws rise above rules. When there is but one exception to the rule it is not a law. (The laws in our Book of Law aren't laws but rules). The laws of energy are predominant and with this insight the apparent control can fall away.

- **Connectedness**
  Connecting will be natural because energies always want to merge with each other. The drive to distinguish and to compare our self, will disappear and will make way for respect and admiration for the beauty of everyone's unique manner of Self-expression. Individualisation as goal to emplace a 'me' will change into giving expression

to Self as a unique link to whole. The form 'Together' no longer exists. Love lets free...

- **Health**
  Sickness will no longer be needed to let us see that we're rowing against the stream. A lot of accidents and chaos will be superfluous because we've already gotten rid of confusion in the energetic layers and this no longer needs to be manifested.
  Thus all manifest will be playing... experimenting... experiencing being human. Always from a deep realisation of the source from where you come. Without guilt, shame or resistance because you know that everything is led from a deeper level; where there is always an agreement with your fellow players.

- **Human capacities**
  We will discover greater human capacities because we are no longer limited to matter and knowledge. We will also teach our children that answers are not in books but in how we can best use the information that is needed from the field of Unity. Where needed there will be knowledge.

Even though there will be a transitory period, once awakened consciousness flows through all of us, the flow of money will no longer be necessary. Because not one of us is one too many. Everything and everyone has a unique role and we keep each other's needs in position. We *are* an equilibrium.

The future vision will be a reality when we open the Now for the Now and we become ourSelves.

VERA

ABOUT VERA

... My eyes are open, but even so I can't see the garden where I stand. The dimension in which I find myself has disappeared and blurred. My third eye sees sharp. A wall. I see a broken wall. The bricks have fallen due to a sudden turn in the road and lie like debris on the ground. The wall is only a framework of a few stones indicating where the wall once stood. It's perfectly clear to me what this metaphor means. My control mechanism has broken down... The wall is a symbol of my ego.

It's the most mundane day you can imagine. The haze dissolves and I look around me. It's seems like the first time I really see the conifers in my backyard. They seem higher, greener and lusher than I remember. For the first time I find them beautiful. It takes my breath away, I'm that impressed. I let my gaze glide over the rest of the garden. The pear tree I planted this spring shows off at the back of the path. His arms proudly spread: powerful through and through. Further on I see the climbing hydrangea in bloom, flowers that never before enchanted me. White and cheerful.

Inside I hear the kids arguing with each other. It doesn't bother me. It's remarkable that it doesn't bother me. There's a sudden calm within me. Wide and full. Warm too. I don't know how I know, but I know for sure that all my trigger points and emotional pain points have just suddenly disappeared.
That night I'm waiting at the chip shop for a family size fries. I look around me and take in all the people, not only their appearance, I also look at the energy around them, letting it go through my scanning channels. One man strikes me the most. He's the type I would have rated as voracious and unconscious before. But now I feel totally ONE with him. There is no more separation between him and me and I can't, try as I might, condemn him. He is me.

Flowers and plants that are suddenly sparkling and full of colour is 'one' thing. What I'm experiencing now surprises me. I feel a strange kind of love for all the people around me. A love that can't be compared to anything. A Love that brings peace and tranquillity. There's no longer a feeling of being alone, being different or being better or less, but only being ONE. What in heaven's name has happened to me?!

For days on end I remain in this experience of oneness. I walk around in a romantic fairy tale where everyone loves everyone else and nature is shrouded in rainbows. I feel one with everything and everyone around

me. There's an understanding of how all the people in my life reflect who I am, who ARE me and I them. Suddenly it seems silly to carry on mulling on things I was so accustomed to doing during my training and work as a psychotherapist. I'm not irritated about anything anymore and live fully in the bliss of the moment.
After several weeks this feeling of love and sparkling life sinks slowly away because I make one big mistake: I want to know what happened to me ...!

But of course I had to find out what happened to me! That's why I can tell you about it now.
At some time you'll be called to return back home. Some people experience this when they've hit rock bottom, others will be given an inkling or a moment or a short time of bliss an yet others see 'home' reflected in something or someone in the outside world. That's how it happened to me, the same as the story above. (Oh yes, all sorts of things happened beforehand and after, but this was the first conscious experience when the mystery revealed itself to me).

Some are amazed at my young age, my four children and want to know which path I followed to find my direction. But everyone's path is different and the only right path to walk is your own path, the one you walk now.
Oh yes, I've also known deep valleys. Cried tea towels full of heartbreak. I've been angry, rebellious, deeply grateful and completely and totally lost.
Until the moment came that everything came to an end... (and new beginnings...)The end of pain and traumas, an end to addictions to the apparent gain of playing roles. The end of experiences that come with a dual life.
Maybe it was because I don't avoid anything, I live everything for the full 100% and don't get attached to anything that doesn't feel right. Maybe it was a reprieve. Certainly these experiences came at the right time and everything that preceded helped to fulfil what I am here for. Everything!

People wonder: why are there so few like you? Well, there's only one like me, and only one like you!
Everyone has a different role, none more or less important than another.
People want to know: is it possible for us to be so light?
The answer is: Yes! It's our birth right.
When all ends dissolve for you, you won't know. But know that every step you take is of value, whether you go left or go right.

MORE INFORMATION

Vera Helleman holds online webinars and meetings in the Netherlands, Belgium and several other countries, in which the transition from ego driven life to effortlessly being yourSelf stands central and in which you can ask personal questions.

A practical online course has also been launched where you as a group enter into a sixty days Self-inquiry. On a daily basis you will be encouraged to integrate this information by completing exercises. Furthermore, you may ask questions and share in a forum.

More information can be found on the website:
www.verahelleman.com

NOTES

Made in United States
North Haven, CT
09 February 2022